NEBRASKA'S POST OFFICE MURALS

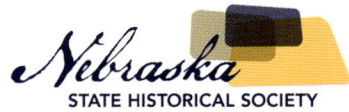

NEBRASKA STATE HISTORICAL SOCIETY BOOKS | LINCOLN

NEBRASKA'S POST OFFICE MURALS

BORN *of the* DEPRESSION, FOSTERED *by the* NEW DEAL

By L. Robert Puschendorf

© 2012 by the Nebraska State
Historical Society, Lincoln
www.nebraskahistory.org

ISBN 978-0-933307-33-9

The paper in this book meets
the guidelines for permanence
and durability of the Committee
on Production Guidelines for
Book Longevity of the Council
on Library Resources, Inc. ∞

Library of Congress
Control Number: 2012942147
Printed in China

Book design by Nathan Putens

Publication of this book was made possible by
James C. and Rhonda Seacrest, Lincoln, Nebraska.

Contents

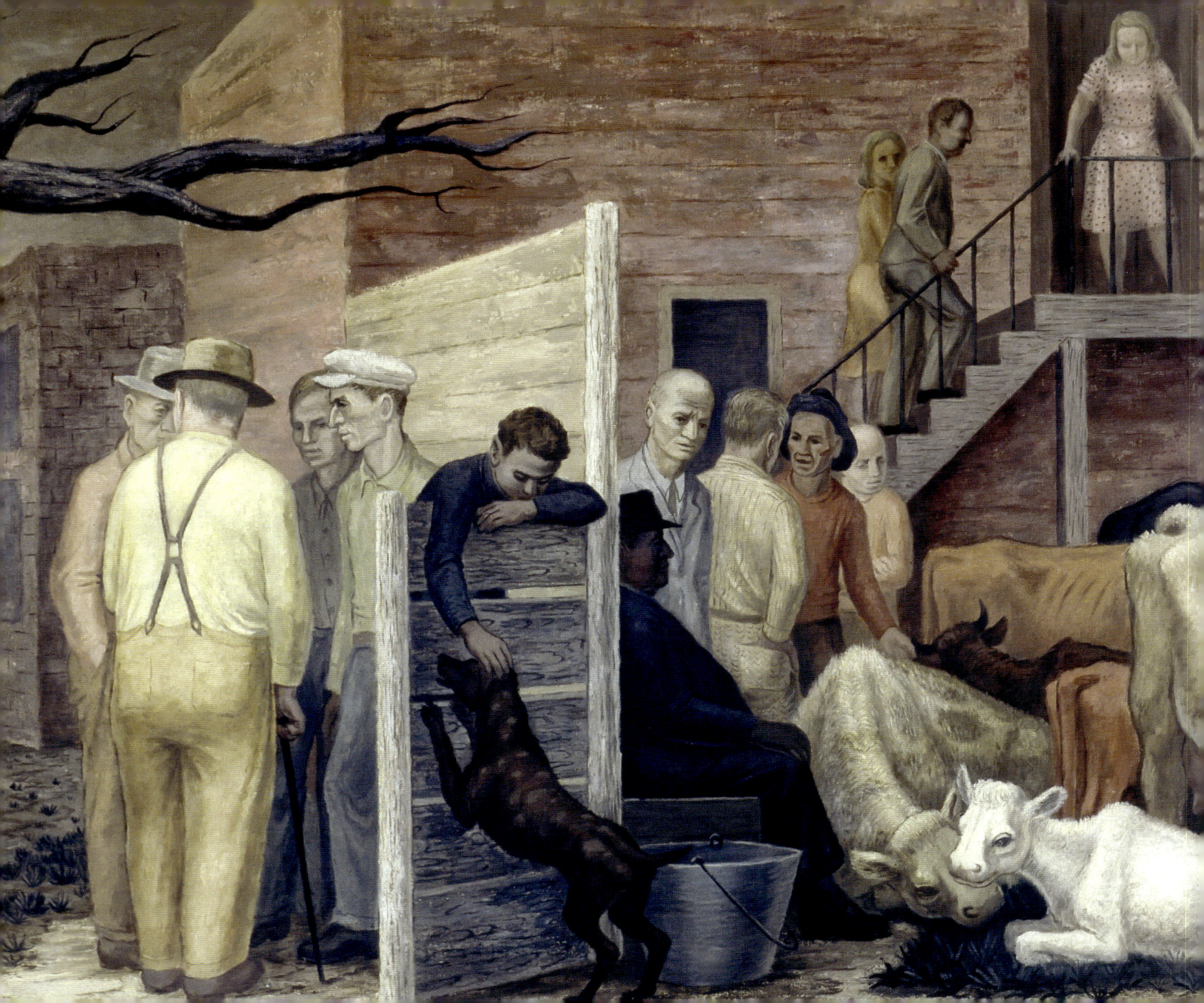

Introduction

Nebraska's twelve post offices that feature murals are part of a national artistic legacy. Three quarters of a century later, they remain a tangible and public link not only to a period of national crisis, but also to that period's ideals. The murals represent an effort to bring art directly to the people — specifically, art that expresses regional identity. American art was coming of age and the murals were presented to a public who had little or no previous exposure to fine arts. They are windows into 1930s American optimism, emphasizing themes of work, history, community, and life on the land, all meant to establish pride in community and a dialogue between the art, the artist, and the public.

But the story of how the murals came to be isn't merely one of artistic vision and governmental beneficence. The art programs themselves were administered by strong personalities who sometimes held opposing visions of what public art should be. The post office mural program involved compromise and an ongoing conversation among artists, administrators, and the public for whom the murals were intended.

Kenneth Evett, *The Auction* (detail),
tempera and oil glaze on canvas, 1942.

Mural Art in the New Deal

*"It was largely a mural art . . . a State-inspired art, born
of the Depression, fostered by the New Deal."*
— Time, 1936

"For the overwhelming majority of the American people, the fine arts of painting and sculpture . . . do not exist," reported a commission appointed by the Hoover administration in 1933. The report went on to say that "[t]here are no indications of direct governmental patronage of the arts to be expected in America in the near future."[1] However, the status of American public art was about to change dramatically.

Following the stock market crash of 1929, huge numbers of U.S. businesses and industries shut down, banks failed, and the nation's financial system virtually collapsed. By 1933, 25 percent of workers were unemployed. Farmers faced foreclosure during an agricultural decline that had begun a decade earlier. The public's outlook was bleak. In his acceptance speech for the 1932 Democratic presidential nomination, Franklin Delano Roosevelt pledged "a new deal for the American people."[2] After taking office the following year, he offered sweeping reforms to address the Great Depression. His "New Deal" redefined the role of government. Among the New Deal's most enduring visual legacies was the federal government's patronage of art.

It began with a letter to the president.

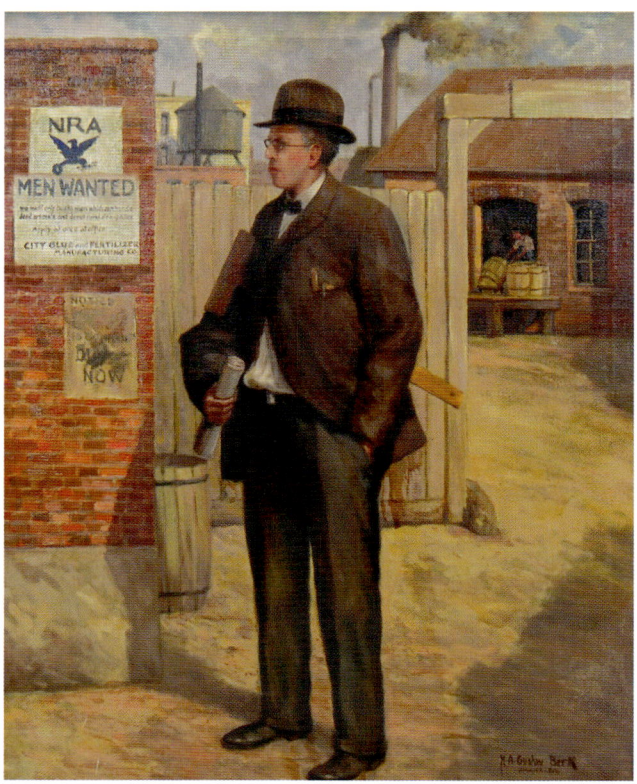

The Forgotten Man, Gustav Berk, oil on canvas. Berk, at the time an unemployed artist from Omaha working for the PWAP, portrayed the plight of a white-collar man searching for work.

George Biddle held the social and political credentials to raise the idea of a public arts program with President Roosevelt. He came from an influential Philadelphia family and was the president's former schoolmate. Following family tradition, Biddle studied law, but soon abandoned it for art. Among his artistic sojourns was Mexico, where he observed a renaissance of mural painting fostered by Mexican President Alvaro Obregón. Here mural painters were paid "plumbers wages," as Biddle put it, to decorate public buildings celebrating traditions of its people, history, and nationalist sentiments.[3] From this program came the artists David Alfaro Siqueiros, José Clemente Orozco, and Diego Rivera.

In a letter to Roosevelt during the first months of the new administration, Biddle noted the achievements of the Mexican art program and suggested a similar program to celebrate the ideals of the New Deal. The idea caught Roosevelt's attention. He referred Biddle to the U.S. Treasury Department, which built and was custodian of federal buildings and had the authority to embellish them with art.

The New Deal is remembered for its "alphabet soup" of federal programs and agencies known by their initials: the WPA, CCC, AAA, NRA, and countless others that came and went, each an experiment in addressing the ongoing economic depression. Among them was the PWAP, the first of several programs established for public art under the New Deal.

The Public Works of Art Project

. . . out of the despair of the spirit.

The Treasury Department's Edward Bruce was described as a "second-string" New Dealer who frequented the influential social and political circles of Washington. A better advocate for public art could not have been found. Bruce made Biddle's idea a reality, leading the first foray into public art to support struggling artists. An international monetary expert, Bruce had recently come to the Treasury Department, but like Biddle he had studied art and had become an artist of some note. Meeting with President Roosevelt, Bruce suggested that some of the newly authorized funding in the Federal Emergency Relief Act be earmarked for art.[4]

Bruce was among many in Washington clamoring for government funds, but he gained support from Harry Hopkins, federal relief administrator and chief architect of the New Deal. Hopkins was enthusiastic, saying of the nation's struggling artists, "Hell! They've got to eat just like other people."[5]

Thus the Public Works of Art Project (PWAP) was established. The U.S. Treasury Department administered the program, using federal relief funds from the Civil Works Administration (CWA), which was established to provide the unemployed with public service jobs during the winter of 1933–34. The agency allocated $3 million to provide work for 2,500 artists.[6]

Bruce had little time to get the project up and running. The CWA and its relief funds would sunset on February 15, 1934. Yet despite typical federal bureaucracy he moved quickly. Sixteen regions of the country were mapped, each overseen by a volunteer committee. Recognized museum directors and other art experts served on these committees and lent credibility to the project. Subcommittees were established at the state level. Some six hundred local and regional volunteers participated in these capacities.[7]

Bruce was now the nation's most prominent proponent of public art. He enlisted Forbes Watson, a well-known art critic, to join the project as technical advisor, and Edward B. Rowan as assistant director. George Biddle, however, shunned a bureaucratic position and continued to practice his art.

The project had two goals: providing relief for the unemployed, and bringing fine arts to the people. PWAP selected artists and paid them a flat weekly rate established by the CWA, defined as "craftsman wages."[8] The agency classified artists into two groups, based both on experience and financial need. More experienced artists were elevated to the top of the pay scale, often without demonstrating financial need.

The agency encouraged its artists to paint in a realistic manner understandable to the public. The art was to make simple statements and stress traditional American values. This style was known as the "American Scene." First labeled as the "American Wave" in the early 1930s, the style was described by the editor of *The Art Digest* as a "movement looking forward to the production of works of art that, avoiding foreign influences, actually expressed the spirit of the land."[9] Some artists believed that art should have a different character from one region to another, reflective of locality and place, history and culture. Among the most notable "regionalist" artists from the Midwest were Grant Wood of Iowa, John Steuart Curry of Kansas, and Thomas Hart Benton of Missouri. Observing the art that came out of the PWAP, Grant Wood stated that the project would lead to the development of a distinctly American school of art:

> In the past few years American artists have been breaking away from the European tradition. The trend was given its greatest stimulus when federal public works directors demanded that native subjects be used wherever possible in art projects . . . We will also see the development of an American method of handling our material . . . In time, American art will be as different from European art as is American life. It is silly to attempt to impose a foreign culture upon America, for if there is to be honest painting and sculpture it will find its origin at home. Culture can't be an imported product.[10]

The country was gradually coming of age culturally. And, as Wood stated, this new artistic style was typically American. The American Scene would become the preferred style of the PWAP and adopted unofficially by the other Treasury programs that would follow. Edward Bruce said "[t]he 'American Scene' was suggested as subject matter, but not insisted upon, the utmost freedom of expression allowed."[11] Although the PWAP promoted the American Scene, some of the works made political and social statements ("Social Realism") when artists focused on candid imagery that drew on the lives of those caught in the reality of the Depression.

Because of the CWA's temporary nature, the PWAP was short-lived. Despite an extension to its funding, the PWAP payroll was cut in half by May 1. It slowed to a halt on June 30, 1934. However, the PWAP employed some 3,750 artists at an estimated cost of $1,312,177. In a final tally, however, nearly half of the artists were not eligible for relief. The project produced 15,663 works consisting of easel paintings, sculptures, watercolors, prints, murals, and mural studies.[12] It also supported craftsmen in iron work, pottery, weaving, wood-carving, and other diverse mediums. Marking the end of the PWAP, selected artworks were displayed at the Corcoran Gallery in Washington, D.C. More than five hundred works were selected for the exhibition, which included examples from every state project.

During its brief existence, PWAP established a relationship between artists and the public. Bruce observed that "[t]here is a desire for beauty, a reaction against the ugliness that surrounds us, a wish to fill one's time with new interests, a hope to find an outlet for the creative spirit." George Biddle said the project "made America art conscious as never before . . . It has made the artist conscious of the fact that he is of service to the community, that he fills a necessary function in our society." As for the quality of the art created Leonard Thiessen, an art critic for the *Omaha World-Herald*, later reflected on public arts projects: "You may think all PWA art lousy. Much of it certainly is. But don't think that government patronage hasn't had a big bolstering effect on the morale of younger artists all over the country."[13]

Elizabeth Olds, *Unskilled Labor Bureau*, lithograph, 1934. Olds's work for the Nebraska PWAP reflected the people's plight during the Depression in the style of "Social Realism."

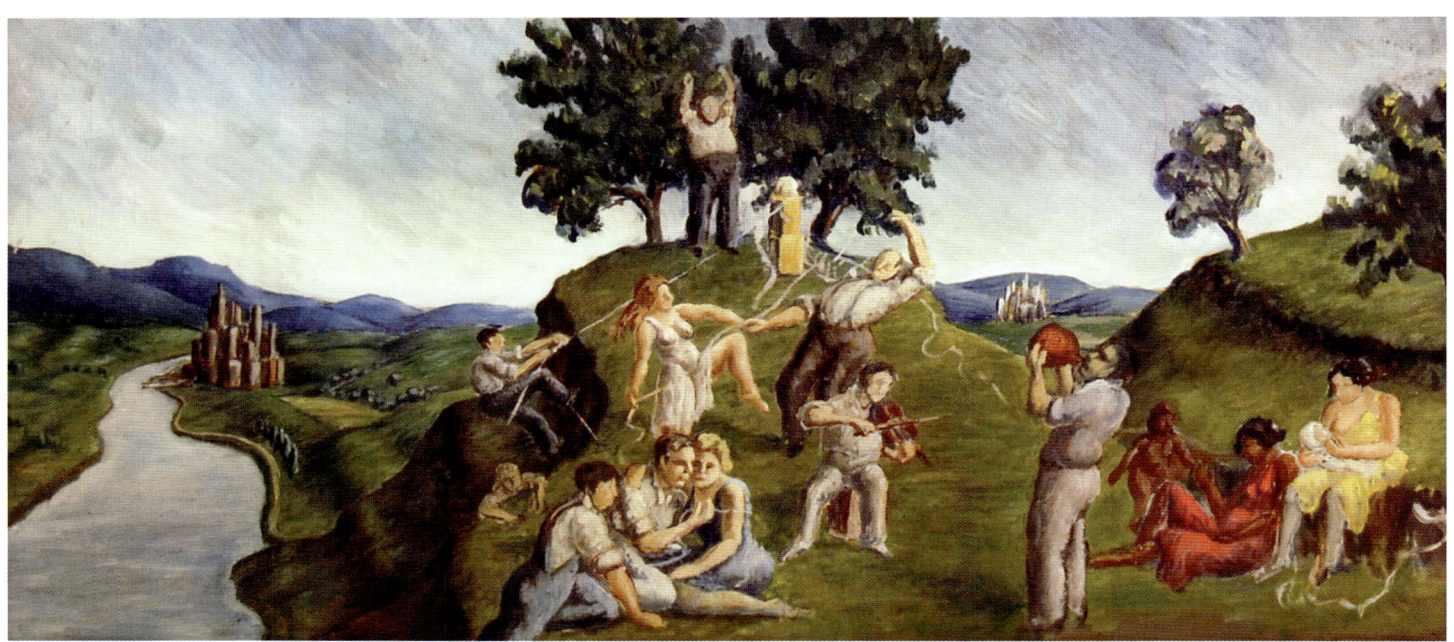

THE NEBRASKA PWAP PROJECT was supervised by Thomas R. Kimball, preeminent Nebraska architect, and Wilda Chace Reeder, Fremont artist and art instructor. Group "A" artists were paid $45 per week; group "B" received $26.50 a week.[14] Some were trained and already well-known in art circles, while others were art students or self-taught. The project attracted several artists who were already well established, such as Elizabeth Dolan, J. Laurie Wallace, and Augustus Dunbier. Perhaps the most prominent artist to gain attention through Nebraska's PWAP program was Elizabeth Olds. A "Social Realist," Olds chose subjects relating the despair of the Depression, including public health clinics, unemployment lines, and homeless men. In all, the PWAP employed thirty-two Nebraska artists.

Because oversight was at the state level, the PWAP reflected the tastes of the supervisors and their preferences for particular schools of art — and the contrast between Iowa and

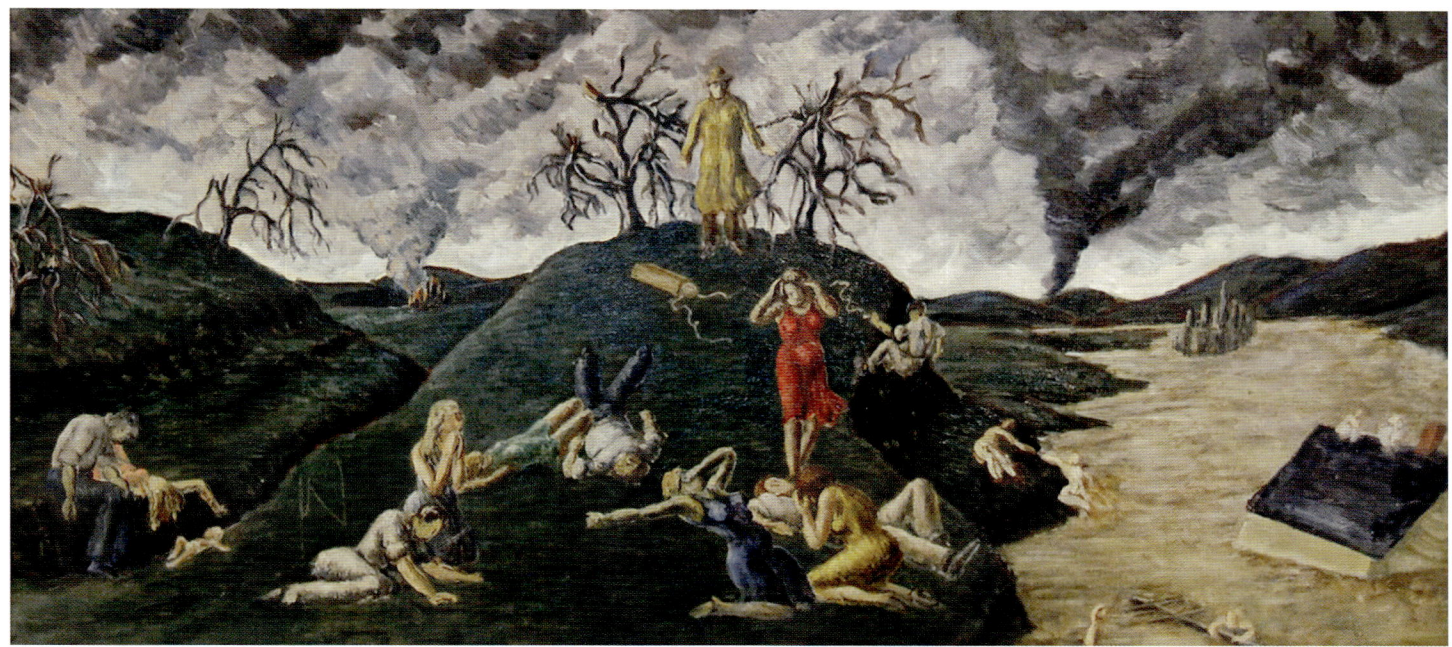

The mural study by John Tazewell Robertson entitled *1929* (*left*), a pre-Depression representation, compares to his sober image, *1933*, (*above*) representing the Depression.

Nebraska was striking. Grant Wood, proponent of the "regionalist" school, supervised the Iowa PWAP. Since Kimball preferred more conservative and traditional art, the two states traded several artists over the course of the project. For example, John Tazewell (Tod) Robertson of Omaha was traded to the Iowa project. Robertson asked for his trade, saying that his tenure in Nebraska was "a flop" because Kimball was not satisfied by his work. The *Omaha World-Herald* called the trade an "old feud between conservatives and moderns."[15]

At issue was a pair of Robertson's mural studies for the new federal building in Omaha, one described by the artist as showing the likeness of Herbert Hoover waving a roast chicken over his head. "This was symbolic of the Republican promises of 1928," Robertson said.[16] Contrasting to this subject, the second study represented the despair of the Depression.

Kimball referred to Robertson's mural studies as "bad art," but the artist later found vindication.[17] In the Corcoran Gallery exhibition meant to celebrate the accomplishments of the PWAP, one of his Missouri River scenes was dubbed the "most representative Nebraska painting" — even though it was painted in Iowa City under Wood's supervision. President and Mrs. Roosevelt then chose the painting to hang in the White House.

Kimball was "puzzled" at the showing of Robertson's work, but PWAP Assistant Director Edward Rowan called the trade "very dignified." Rowan said the work was "an extremely competent, interesting canvas," and added (no doubt to Kimball's chagrin), "Some of the things set [sic] down here from Nebraska I was forced to return as not being at all adequate." Only one Nebraska artist, Sarah Green, was represented in the exhibition with her watercolor, *Winter Blizzard*. For Robertson, who found himself in the middle of the controversy, it was "all very confusing."[18]

The PWAP collections remained in federal ownership, but found homes in publically-supported institutions. Nebraska's PWAP works were given on permanent loan to the Nebraska State Historical Society at the close of the project, including examples of 190 easel paintings, prints, batiks, posters, and several mural studies.[19] Governor Charles W. Bryan selected five of the works for the governor's mansion.

Ernest Witte, administrator of the Nebraska Emergency Relief Agency, wrote, "We seldom think of Nebraska as the home of much artistic endeavor and yet we discovered a wealth of talent and ability."[20] In fact, he indicated that one artist who produced the finest work was untrained. Overall,

> [T]he government which is continually concerned with the promotion of material welfare . . . gave recognition to the creative and artistic urges of its citizens and promoted art . . . it developed an idea which not only allowed these individuals to earn their daily bread, but stimulated interests and ambitions in their own field and took them out of the despair of the spirit.[21]

Although the PWAP received criticism, it stimulated support for large-scale government patronage of the arts. The short-lived program had significance as the first art project subsidized by the federal government on a national scale. Art had a new patron.

The WPA

A new deal for artists

With its massive public works projects, the WPA (Works Progress Administration, later the Works Projects Administration) was among the best known New Deal programs. It resulted from the huge Federal Emergency Relief Appropriation Act of 1935 and included two WPA art projects. One was an extensive project of arts and humanities for the unemployed. Another would employ artists to decorate federal buildings. These two projects represented a new deal for artists.

In May 1935 the president asked Edward Bruce and Harry Hopkins, administrator of the newly created WPA, to work out what became two programs for unemployed artists. Hopkins established a full-scale relief program for artists, the WPA Federal Art Project (FAP). The largest of the New Deal art projects, FAP was established in August 1935 and operated on a massive scale supporting artists eligible for relief. "Federal Project Number One," known simply as "Federal One," established programs for the visual arts, music, theater, and writing. It was highly decentralized, with state directors assigned from art galleries or museums, art associations, and universities. The Nebraska project apparently had difficulty finding a state sponsor. Six states, including Nebraska, were supervised directly by the WPA when a state director couldn't be found. In January 1939 ten states had no such projects, including Nebraska.[22]

By contrast Bruce's plan, the Treasury Relief Art Project (TRAP), had only limited requirements as a relief program. This provision reflected Bruce's priorities for quality work.

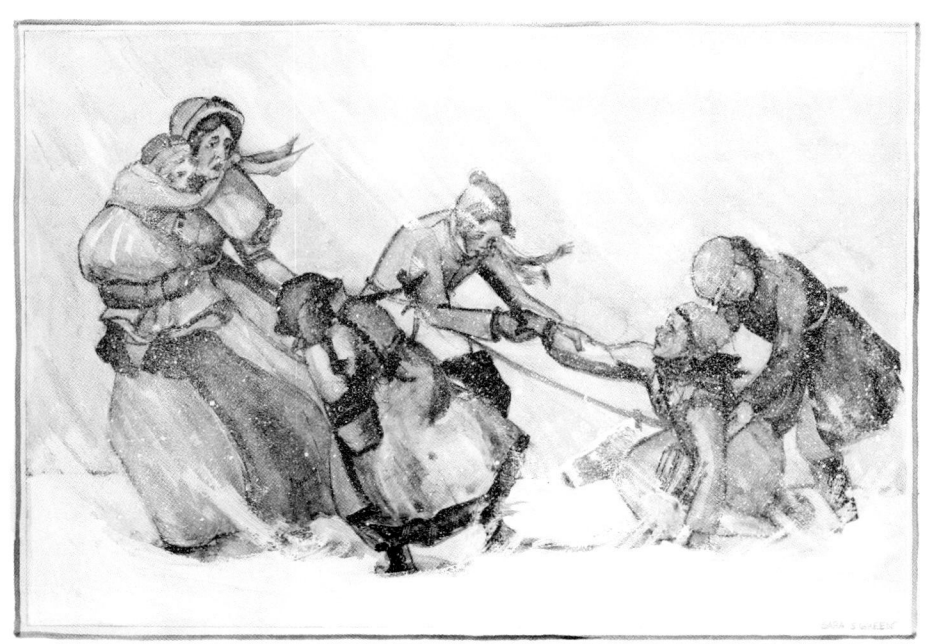

Sarah Green's watercolor, *Winter Blizzard*, is an example of the American Scene. It depicts a historical incident—the Blizzard of 1888—and a teacher taking her students to safety. From a 1934 photograph.

When asked to head up the FAP, he refused, thinking that a relief program would sacrifice artistic quality.[23] Encouraged by PWAP's relative success, Bruce had already proposed establishing a permanent Treasury Department division for the embellishment of federal buildings. Treasury Secretary Henry Morgenthau, Jr., authorized the Section of Painting and Sculpture in a departmental order of October 16, 1934. Bruce became its chief administrator. The Section of Painting and Sculpture (later the Section of Fine Arts) became known simply as "the Section."

In its first announcement, C. J. Peoples, director of procurement for the Public Works Branch of the Treasury, captured what would become the Section's purpose:

> Without being sentimental, the Section of Painting and Sculpture hopes that in employing the vital talents of this country, faith in the country and a renewed sense of its glorious possibilities will be awakened both in the artists and in their audiences, and that through this Section will do its full share in the development of the art and the spiritual life of the United States of America.[24]

The Treasury Relief Art Project

The "Ritz" of the public art projects

The Treasury Relief Art Project (TRAP) began in July 1935 as a project of the Section, which soon established an operating plan anticipating the employment of four to five hundred artists.

As a WPA project, TRAP followed the rules of relief, but quality of work was paramount. According to a bulletin released by the Section, the project was

> to employ experienced artists who are on relief, in the making of murals, sculpture and individual pictures for federal buildings . . . [A]ll of this work must meet standards of high professional competency and distinguished quality as art . . . There are no special quotas for states and the policy will be to obtain the best art possible wherever it exists.[25]

Edward B. Rowan, formerly PWAP's assistant director and named as superintendent of the Section, began by taking the old PWAP artist files and arranging them into three groups marked "good, medium, and bums."[26]

Under WPA rules, 90 percent of TRAP's artists were to be from relief rolls (this was later reduced to 75 percent). Wages varied from $69 to $103 a month, which was the "going wage" for comparably skilled, professional workers under WPA pay schedules.[27] Also employed — though not necessarily on the basis of relief — were "master" artists, who included practicing and professional artists. Many of the master artists oversaw the quality of work, administered local projects, interviewed artists, monitored relief rules and compliance, and reported on the project's activities.

As for the art itself, possible locations were many. The works would embellish federal buildings, either new buildings or those that had not received art. The Treasury Department held nearly $145 million to build 233 federal buildings, including post offices, federal courthouses and office buildings, marine hospitals, and immigration stations.[28] While TRAP produced murals and sculpture, most of its works were easel paintings, watercolors, posters, prints, and the "decorative."

The Section took examples of this work directly to the public through traveling exhibitions for schools, colleges, art galleries, public libraries, and other public institutions. A 1936 exhibition of twenty-two watercolors produced under TRAP was shown at the Joslyn Memorial, Omaha's new arts and cultural center.[29]

In Nebraska, the project struggled to find suitable artists on relief rolls. Prominent Nebraska artist Augustus Dunbier inquired of Olin Dows, chief of the Treasury Relief Art Project, "in order that we may start the wheels rolling." Neighboring Kansas and Iowa already had established projects. Olin Dows had previously telegraphed Dwight Kirsch, chairman of the Department of Fine Arts at the University of Nebraska and secretary of the Nebraska Art Association, requesting a list of Nebraska artists on relief. Kirsch replied by letter that "you will probably not find great numbers of talented artists in Nebraska who are unemployed at present."[30]

Dows agreed: "I am sure that there are very few artists on relief now in the country who are talented . . . It is those persons I want to find." From a list of nine unemployed artists provided by the state director of the National Reemployment Service, Kirsch thought only two had potential. But he confided to Dows that the efforts failed "to bring forth any promising material for your project," and suggested three other artists who were not on relief. Dows, however, rejected them because "this project has to stick very closely to relief, and I am afraid at the moment that I shall be unable to start any project in Nebraska unless I can find artists on relief who are sufficiently capable."[31] In the end, no Nebraska project was represented in TRAP.

TRAP is often confused with the WPA Federal Art Project, which was denigrated as a simple "make work" program for less talented artists. Despite its relief requirements, a *Time* magazine article called TRAP "the Ritz" of the public art projects, saying "TRAP artists look down their noses at their WPA brethren." As Forbes Watson, art critic and technical advisor to the Treasury's Section of Painting and Sculpture, explained, "WPA's main point is relief. Ours is art."[32]

TRAP was a short-lived program; the government began to phase it out by the end of 1936. It employed 356 artists at its peak, but only 135 by the end of June 1937. In all, it produced 89 murals and 65 sculpture projects, plus 10,000 easel paintings.[33]

Most of the former TRAP artists transferred to WPA projects. Some of those who were on relief found work through the WPA's FAP, which continued to produce art, performances, music, and literature until the late years of the New Deal public works programs.

The Section

". . . glorious possibilities . . ."

The most significant project for public murals and sculptures in federal buildings again found its home in the Treasury's Section of Painting and Sculpture. It was dedicated to providing artworks for newly constructed federal buildings, including post offices.

Treasury Secretary Morgenthau's 1934 directive said the Section was "to secure suitable art of the best quality available for the embellishment of public buildings." It would "make every effort to afford an opportunity to all artists on the sole test of their qualifications as artists."[34]

For artists of both known and emerging talent, the Section offered an outlet for their works and a connection with their audience. And for the public, the project would "carry out this work in such a way as will assist in stimulating, as far as practicable, development of art in this country."[35] An enthusiastic Bruce stated, "We owe it to the government to make this movement so important that it is going to ring around the world . . . We shall become aware increasingly that as artists we are working not only as individuals, but as indispensable parts of a great nation-wide cooperative plan."[36]

Unlike TRAP, the Section's program was centralized in Washington to ensure control over the production of artwork. It would select artists who showed competence through competitions, avoiding the constraints attached to the relief projects. The competition system also minimized controversy in the selection process, and ensured that untalented artists were weeded out, while those demonstrating talent would have opportunities for other commissions. Certain artists could be selected "because of their recognized talent, [and] entitled to receive work without competition."[37] Thus, the process offered the selection of both well-established artists and talented newcomers to the art scene, supposedly without prejudice or favoritism.

A People's Audience

"The mural . . . belongs to a people's audience."

The Section's goal was to place art before the public in places most accessible to local citizens. It saw public art as a connection between the artist and the public. As one artist explained, "the mural, by virtue of its physical characteristics (being of large scale on a wall where it is on permanent public display), belongs to a people's audience."[38]

The works presented familiar subjects in a simple and direct manner. Since the Section wanted authentic subject matter related to the locale, the murals were more regional than works from of other federal arts projects. The American Scene dominated mural commissions. Themes meant to inspire by presenting familiar subjects far from the realities of the Depression. According to Section administrator Edward Bruce, "fine murals, concerned with the locality and by artists of the region, placed in public buildings, stimulate local culture. Through these wall pictures, everyday scenes, familiar objects, industries, etc., achieve a new dignity." A bulletin issued by the Section later observed, "There is no doubt that some of our most distinguished murals are by artists who have really studied the life, past or present, of the place for which their murals were designed."[39] Thus, the Section sought artists or works with familiarity with the locales for which the murals were intended.

The Post Office Murals

A "concrete link . . ."

Post offices were the logical choice for presenting art to the people. And what better place? The post office was where the local community congregated socially and conducted business daily. Especially in smaller towns, original professional-quality art was seldom seen. Bruce recognized the potential. "The post office . . . is the one concrete link between every community of individuals and the Federal Government . . . [it] functions importantly in the human structure of the community."[40] And Forbes Watson asked:

> When the farmer, the laborer, the village children and the storekeepers go to the nearest Post Office and see there, for example, a distinguished work of contemporary art depicting the main activities, or some notable events in the history of the town, is it too exaggerated to suggest that their interest will be increased and their imaginations stirred?[41]

The Treasury Department launched a building campaign of unprecedented scale, which included hundreds of new post offices, giving many opportunities for the placement of art. It is estimated that more than three times the number of post offices were constructed in the decade of the New Deal as during the previous fifty years.[42]

When the Federal Relief Appropriation Act of 1935 became law, Bruce announced in the Treasury's bulletin:

> Next year the Treasury Department will put up many federal buildings. A large proportion of these will be federal post offices of a local order. The amounts allocated to them for painting and sculpture will be comparatively small but I feel sure that these buildings will afford fine opportunities for our painters and our sculptors and they should be quick to take advantage of them.[43]

Only new post offices would receive murals or wall-mounted sculptures. Although Bruce had advocated a one percent allocation for art, each new building instead was given a reserve for overruns in the construction budget. Buildings that came in at or over their construction budget would not receive artwork. But if the reserve wasn't needed, then about one percent could be authorized for a mural or sculpture.

Because of their relative costs, mural commissions outnumbered those for sculpture. Common subject matter included depictions of the postal service or scenes related to the community — such as small town life, people at work on farms and industries, and local history and folklore. One of the most popular mural subjects was local history, often drawing from sometimes questionable local lore (as with the WPA's Federal Writers' Project, which cranked out reams of paper on these subjects). The murals followed the historical interpretations of the day. Today's historians may critique their accuracy — and stereotypes — but the murals stand as products of their time.

The Section claimed that it didn't want to stifle artistic expression. As Bruce stated in 1934, the objective was "to keep away from official art and to develop local cultural interests throughout the country." Its instructions included a standard notice that "in promoting American artists [the Section] is not interested in promoting any one particular school of painting, but in giving every American artist an equal chance."[44]

In reality, however, the Section encouraged the American Scene — in practice if not through established standards. Though it specified no specific style, it sought to make the works understandable and acceptable to local audiences by encouraging realism. Likewise, the Section had little interest in the allegorical and mythical figures of classicism, and it discouraged the political and ideological themes of the Social Realists, along with subject matter that portrayed the strength of the federal government, and avant-garde styles such as Surrealism, Cubism, or abstract art. The result, without the Section ever asking for it directly, was the American Scene.

The Section wanted murals that exuded optimism to the public, unconnected to their plight during the Depression. After all, the Depression was seen as temporary and the murals would be lasting. And since many artists were practicing in the realistic styles popular during the period, the Section had a large body of artists from which to choose. Artists familiar with the judges' preferences, however, admitted they sometimes put aside other subject matter or a preferred artistic style to "paint Section."[45] Artist Kenneth Evett later recalled in an interview:

> The subject matter was not demanded but I think the Federal authorities were also involved in that whole regionalist phobia and we were all painting the pony express and scenes of local history, themes having to do with glorification of the American past. I did the same kind of thing.[46]

The Section announced competitions in bulletins edited by Forbes Watson, which eventually reached an audience of 8,500 artists by 1938. An artist could receive blueprints showing the spaces proposed for the particular building. The Section recommended that the artist take into account the surroundings for which the mural was destined, such as "the color and substance of the walls, the shape, size and proportion of any openings or other structural incidents adjacent to, or cutting into, the proposed mural." In doing so, the committee of judges could "realize how well [the artist] has understood the problem facing him."[47]

Fewer than 15 of the 190 competitions were national; these were reserved for the most monumental of federal buildings, including those being built in the nation's capital. C. J. Peoples, Treasury's director of procurement, said the Section would seek "the ablest artists in America to do the work regardless of their place of residence . . . [and]

to select work which shall be able to stand up against the severest critical examination of artists and laymen alike."[48]

Regional competitions for federal buildings of less prominence were open to artists "resident of, or attached to" states in the general region of the commission.[49] These competitions, therefore, leaned toward artists with familiarity of the area and knowledge of appropriate local subject matter.

Competition rules required artists to submit designs that were unsigned and unidentified. After a local jury made its recommendations, the designs were sent to the Section for a decision. The artist's identity was not revealed until after the final selection.

In addition, runners-up for competitions would have a chance to be considered for lesser commissions in local post offices. In its first bulletin, the Section explained:

> Without in any way lowering the standard for which we desire to maintain, in even the least of our painting and sculpture projects, we do want through them to bring to a larger public notice natively strong artists who hitherto have had no opportunity to win such notice. In a word, we look to what we have called our "local" projects for the discovery and development of hitherto comparatively unknown artists who will be able, in carrying out these less complex undertakings, to prove their right to be invited by the Section to design murals and execute sculpture for the great buildings which the government has erected in various large centers of the country.[50]

These commissions were based on what the Section called "competent" designs. For many, winning a particular competition was less important than gaining the Section's attention, which could lead to a post office commission. In 1940 Bruce reported that of the 572 artists who received commissions, 184 were competition winners, but 382 were selected from the "competent" submittals.[51] Kenneth Evett, a young artist who went on to produce Section murals (including one for the post office in Pawnee City, Nebraska), recalled that "we entered practically every available competition that came along and in no time at all even though God knows we weren't really ready for it, we were painting murals." And both the competition system and the chance of being selected for lesser commissions created opportunities for women artists and minorities, many of whom had found themselves overlooked in the art world. More than one sixth of the artists who worked for the Section were women.[52]

Older artists, however, sometimes found the system frustrating. After completing his first mural in 1934 under the Public Works of Art Project, Archie Musick competed unsuccessfully for six years before receiving a commission for the post office in Red Cloud, Nebraska. Though only in his late thirties, he wrote to Rowan:

> [W]hat about us older ones who were born some fifteen years too soon to enjoy the opportunities afforded the younger painters now — many of them in their early twenties . . . Objectively I have felt the pathos of older school literary painters too stubborn to open their minds to encroaching structural requirements, too blind to foresee their own eventual submergence.[53]

Despite the Section's efforts to judge proposals by quality, the works were not always well received. Regarding a 1937 exhibition of mural studies at the Joslyn Memorial, an *Omaha World-Herald* art critic said that it "looks as though it might be intended to illustrate all the degrees of good and bad in mural art. In spite of the care which was supposed to be to be exercised in the selection of painters to do murals, many of the designs are certainly not outstanding examples of mural art . . . There have been very few great mural painters in history, so it is unlikely that the government will 'discover' many under the present project."[54] But despite the perceptions of quality and talent, the Section nevertheless revealed some of the finest talents of all the federal art projects.

Time magazine lauded the Treasury's program, saying the U.S. government had become "the world's No. 1 patron of painting. Federal art lovers may or may not be right in thinking this patronage will be the most fruitful since the Medicis, but in one respect at least it has encouraged a Renaissance."[55]

Art and Architecture

"...one complete architectural unit."

The challenge of commissioning art for hundreds of post offices was complicated by the buildings' standardization. Starting in 1914, the Treasury Department implemented what Secretary of the Treasury William McAdoo described as "a rational system of uniformity and business economy in designing and constructing public buildings, so that buildings suitable to the public needs may be built without waste of Government money." At the same time, the system was intended to produce "buildings adapted to local conditions and in keeping with the importance of the communities in which they are to be erected." It established four classes of post office buildings. "Class A" and "Class B" were the largest and most prominent post offices, designed with quality materials and interior public spaces with "monu-

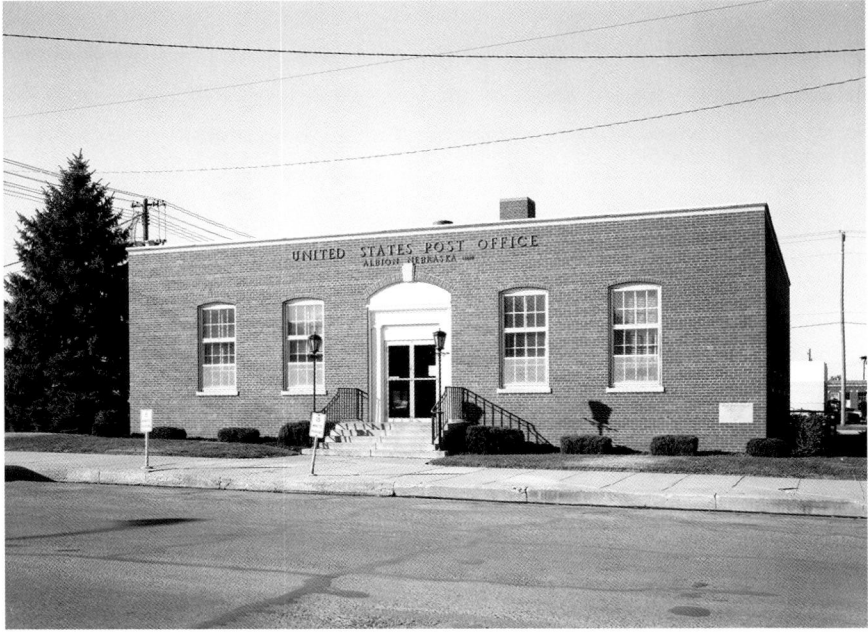

One of the smallest and most modest of the Nebraska post offices is in Albion, built in 1937–38 and reflecting the Treasury's long-standing preference for a "sensible, utilitarian character."

mental treatment." Class "A" would include spaces for "mural decorations." "Class C" post offices had brick facing with stone or terra cotta on the exterior. Public spaces had fewer decorative features with limited use of more expensive wood and marble, and were "restricted to very simple forms of ornament." "Class D" was the most modest classification. These post offices would have brick facing and little stone or terra cotta trim. The buildings were ones "such as any business man would consider a reasonable investment in a small town."[56]

After a hiatus of public building construction during World War I, the Treasury Department slowly reestablished a program of constructing federal buildings. Congress vastly increased funding for a building program in 1930, shortly after the great stock market crash of the previous October.

In 1931, two years before Franklin Roosevelt took office and established the New Deal, the Federal Employment Stabilization Act began to hire unemployed architects or struggling architectural firms, supplementing those of the Supervising Architect's office, which was increased to a staff of almost eight hundred. Appropriations for public buildings were increased by $100 million.[57]

Under the huge emergency relief programs of the New Deal, standardized plans became a priority to keep up with the explosion of post office construction. The peak year of construction, 1937, saw 303 post offices built. The Treasury Department attempted to authorize post offices in every Congressional district, probably to garner support from public officials.[58]

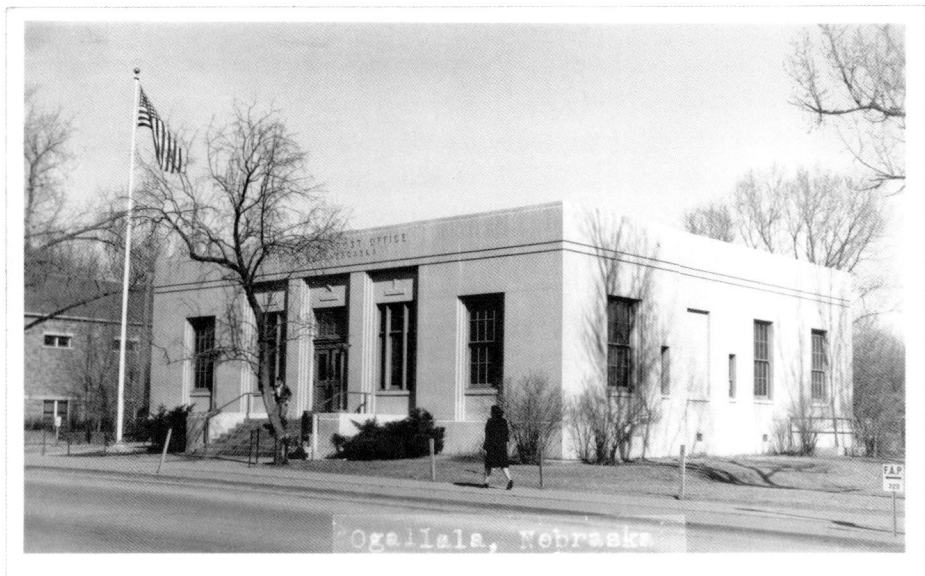

The Ogallala, Nebraska, post office reflects the Moderne style. Three stylized panels above the central windows and entrance depict postal transportation: an airplane, railroad locomotive, and steamship.

The Treasury continued its long-standing policy of standardized plans, producing a set of "cabinet sketches" for the design of smaller post offices. And in keeping with the department's policy, post offices were of a "sensible, utilitarian character instead of the monumental edifices."[59] The Treasury's report for fiscal year 1937 stated:

A large portion of the program has consisted of small post office buildings spread over the entire United States. Type designs were developed, and in order to meet the varying requirements of the Post Office Department and the sectional architectural traditions 11 designs were required. By thus standardizing the designs, there resulted in a great saving in time and cost of production of the drawings and specifications, and the placing of these projects on the market was greatly expedited. The buildings which have been constructed for these type designs have proved economical and satisfactory.[60]

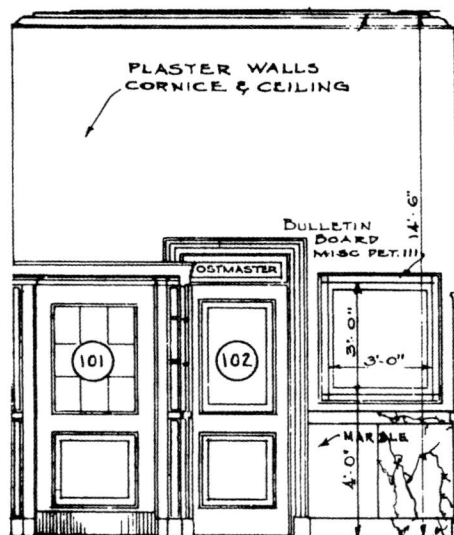

The mural is to be 12'2" wide x 6' 9" high, with a total approximate area of 84 square feet. The mural is to be located on the end wall of the public lobby over the Postmaster's door.

The wainscot is Ozark Grey Veined marble; the color of the walls is a light warm buff; the ceiling is a light cream. The floor is terrazzo marble chips of alternate blocks of (1) Green and Grey Tennessee marble; and (2) Medium Pink Tennessee marble, Cardiff Green and Black. The border is Texas Black and Texas Blue marble chips.

A drawing of the interior elevation of the Schuyler, Nebraska, post office shows the typical placement proposed for a mural and the entrance vestibule (see detail 101) that jutted into the lobby. Section of Fine Arts, Bulletin #19, June 1939.

Thus the design for the Valentine, Nebraska, post office is nearly identical to the one in Fredericktown, Missouri; both were built in 1936–37.

Standardized plans for interiors left little room for change, but allowed some architectural latitude for exteriors. These featured architectural styles ranging from a simplified Classical style, to Colonial Revival to Moderne. All featured symmetrical front facades, which in some cases received embellishment with bronze grillwork and American eagles above the entrance. Some featured stylized panels representing modes of postal transportation, such as airplanes, trains, and steamships.

Bruce lauded the cooperation between architects and mural artists in his milestone 1936 book, *Art in Federal Buildings*, co-authored with Forbes Watson. Since the program was placed in the Office of the Supervising Architect, Bruce said that "cooperation between the architects, painters and sculptors employed by the Program can be developed to its highest point. . . [t]he present program is the first one completely organized to combine painting and sculpture with architecture in a coherent production unit. This cooperation between the three great arts is what gives this program its essential character of permanence and its social and educational force."[61]

This claim may have been true for the monumental buildings constructed in Washington, D.C., and elsewhere, including those where spaces were reserved for murals or sculpture, but the standardized designs that were being cranked out for the smaller classes of post offices placed limitations on where the mural could be located within the building. "[W]e are having a hell of a time with the architects in providing mural spaces. They are dead set against this whole program," said an exasperated Bruce. "Look at the spaces in the post

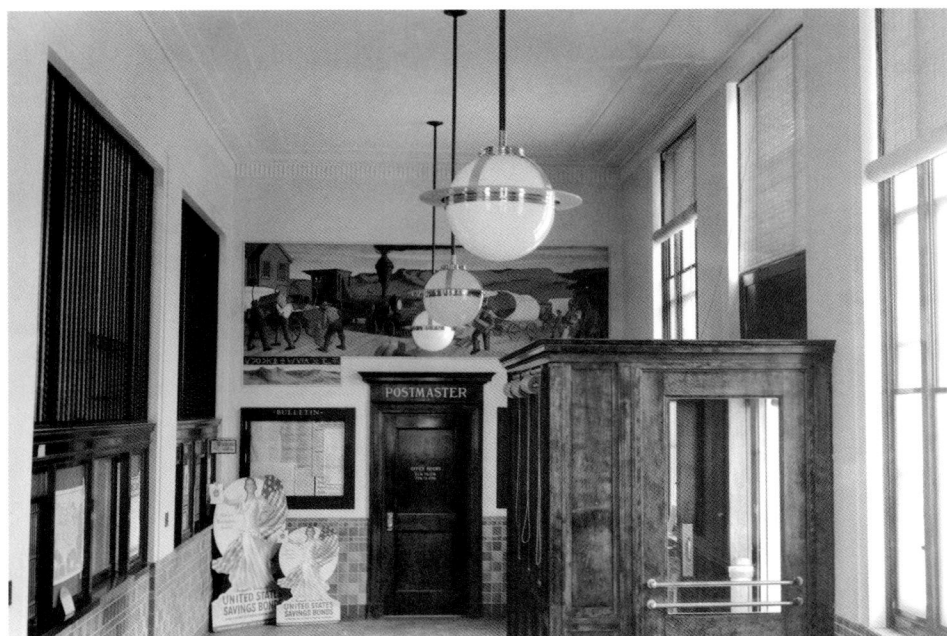

A 1939 photograph of the lobby of the Valentine, Nebraska, post office shows the hanging light fixtures and the entrance vestibule.

offices and you can see what rotten spaces they are. 99% of our work goes in the post offices."[62]

Indeed, the interiors were not designed for murals, nor did the standardized plans offer any provision for the placement of art. In addition, funds for art could not be set aside until the building was 75 percent completed.[63] Therefore, it wasn't known that a particular post office would even be chosen for a mural until it was clear that funds remained from the building's construction reserve.

In employing standardized floor plans, the smaller post offices had long, narrow public lobbies some forty-two feet long and twelve to fourteen feet wide. The mural would have to be placed high above the door to the postmaster's office, which was flanked by two glass-encased bulletin boards. And the narrow lobbies were interrupted by an entry vestibule that jutted into the space, making it difficult to view the murals from a distance. Some artists felt that the spaces were uninspiring and encouraged mediocrity. Despite the limitations, the Section was committed to placing murals in these spaces.

Artists could receive blueprints so they could get an idea of the lobby space and the position of the wall where the mural would be placed. Colors of the marble trim, floor, and woodwork were sometimes described so that the artist could introduce a complementary color scheme. Mary Pollard Hull, an art critic for the *Omaha World-Herald*, said that challenges arose "directly from the fact that murals are really architectural decorations, rather than individual paintings. The color, for instance, must work toward decorative harmony, and the subject of a mural picture must be appropriate to the character of the building without becoming too commonplace."[64]

The mural typically ran about five or six feet in height above the postmaster's office door. In length, the mural spanned the width of the lobby. Artists used different methods to address this limitation. For example, they might cut around the top of the doorway and carry the design down to the tops of the bulletin boards. Rowan wrote:

> In reviewing a number of murals done under this program . . . I arrived at the conclusion that . . . rectangular panels are sometimes difficult to relate architecturally to the other features of the wall. It is suggested that a color tone taken from the mural or harmonizing with it be carried around the door and bulletin boards making one complete architectural unit of the mural wall.[65]

Artists might also simplify the design so viewers could read the painting from well below. They could also compress the visual field to accommodate the reality of the flat wall surface. One art critic wrote, "A painting ordinarily should create an illusion of third dimension, or distance in depth, but in mural painting this illusion must not be so convincing as to destroy the flatness of the wall, nor yet so unconvincing as to lose pictorial depth." And in describing the subject matter, Olin Dows, head of the Treasury Relief Art Project, cautioned, "There are many crowded sketches. There is a definite tendency to insert many incidents in each composition, with consequent artificial dividing up of the composition and insertion of incidents at various scales. This is not often successful."[66]

Light fixtures — globes hung by a chain from the lobby ceiling — were the bane of both the artist and the Section. The fixtures obscured the view of the mural. The artist was given a questionnaire to address his or her concern about the light fixtures. Due to Treasury Department bureaucracy, the fixture's chain could be shortened but only after a lengthy correspondence through departmental channels and the need to procure bids for the work. An exasperated Bruce proclaimed that if "it takes thirty tons of blueprints to make a battleship, why does it take twenty tons of blueprints to make a simple little light fixture in a Post Office?"[67]

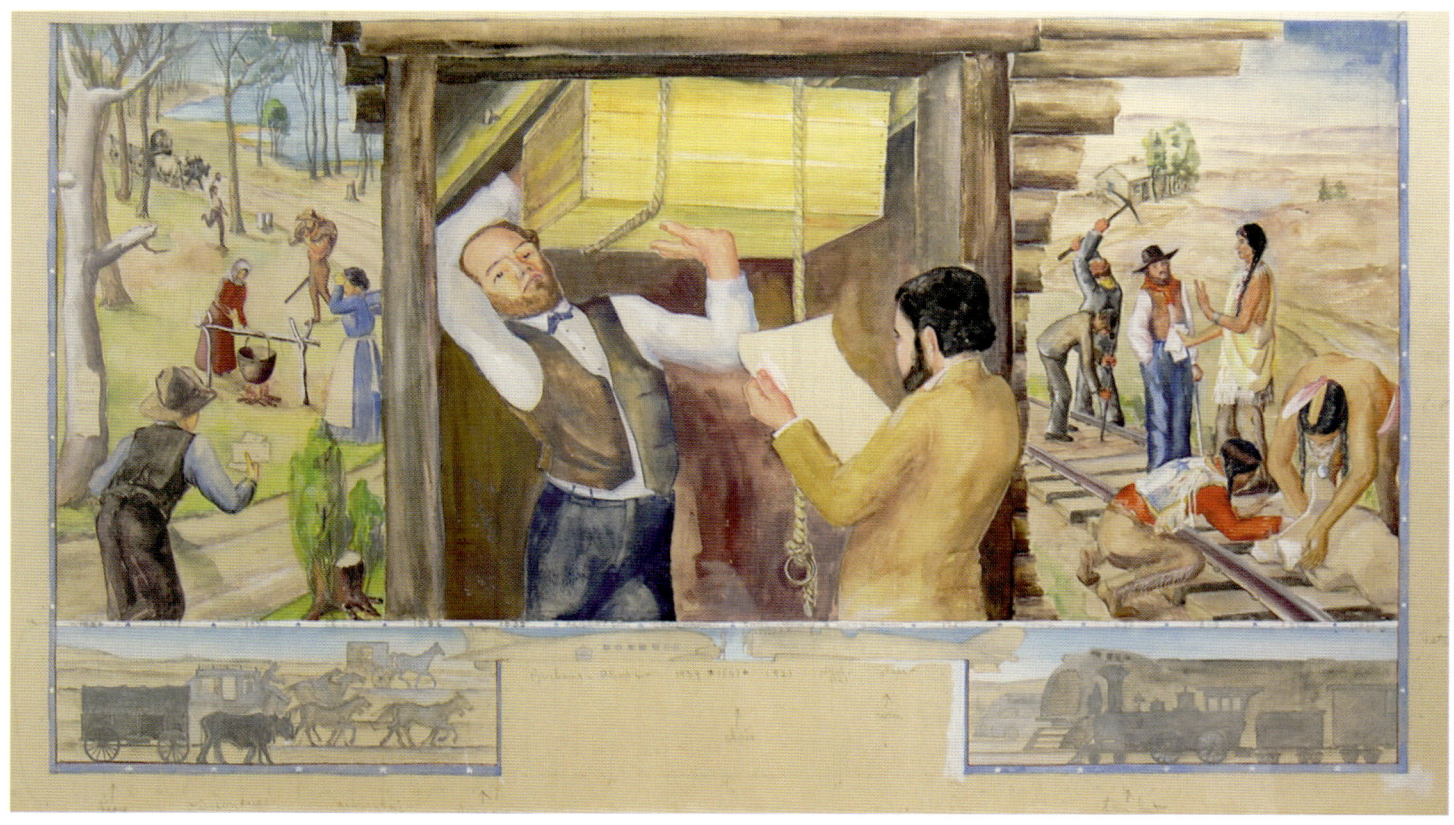

One Nebraska artist who submitted an unsuccessful entry for the Schuyler, Nebraska, post office was Gladys Lux of Lincoln, an artist and art instructor at Nebraska Wesleyan University. It presented a complex range of activities which was not in keeping with the need to make a mural readily understandable.

The Correspondence Course

"We are, in fact, their champions."

Once an artist contracted with the Section, the subsequent process has been described as a "correspondence course" in painting for the public. One artist described the process as "hurry up and wait."[68] Section Superintendent Edward B. Rowan produced most of the volumes of correspondence, adding his recommendations for subject matter, artistic style, and sometimes the minutest details. He was an art historian, artist, and former member of Grant Wood's Stone City Art Colony, where he became a proponent of regionalism. Leonard Thiessen, Nebraska artist and one-time art critic for the *Omaha World-Herald*, commented on the Section's oversight: "Treasury division murals, like all official art, have very definite limitations, [and] must be as squawk-proof as possible. Too uncompromising realism is apt to bring instructions from Washington to 'fatten up the farmers and give them a pleasant smile.'"[69]

Some artists valued the comments; others were more resistant. But since payment was based on satisfactory completion of the mural, most artists complied dutifully. Eldora Lorenzini entered into the Section's "correspondence course" when she submitted mural sketches for the Hebron, Nebraska, post office. Even after receiving the commission, it took Lorenzini many revisions — along with pointed comments and coaching by the Section — before her mural was authorized to be installed more than a year later.

But although the works were frequently critiqued, Rowan respected the artist and tried to be constructive. "We are, in fact, their champions," he wrote.[70] Correspondence often became personal. Lighthearted discussion of family affairs, experience of trips to post office locations, and news of mutual acquaintances showed familiar relationships that developed between Rowan and the artists.

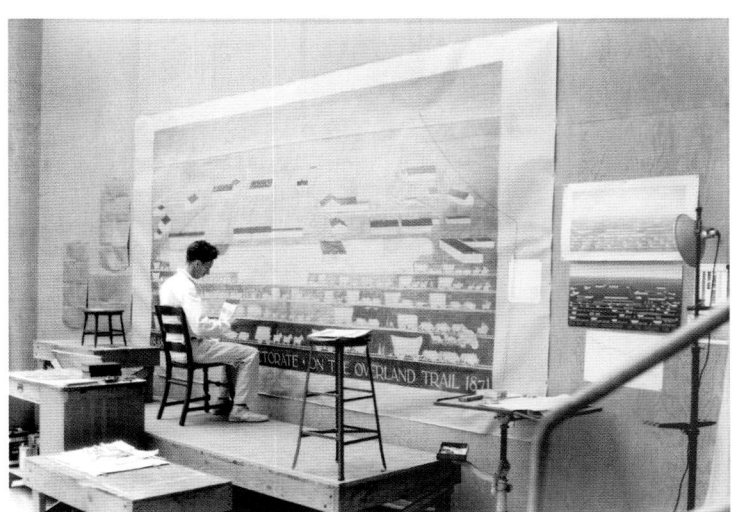

William E. L. Bunn working on his mural for the Minden, Nebraska, post office.

Although the Section estimated the cost of a mural at ten to twenty dollars a square foot (based on commercial rates), Rowan reported that most murals cost between $500 and $700, or about $15 a square foot.[71] When Frank Mechau — then commissioned for the post office in Ogallala, Nebraska — questioned the amount, Rowan replied, "As you know, approximately one percent of the total limit of cost of a building may be reserved for decoration of a building . . . We are aware that the program is not ideally perfect but I think that you are convinced that we are doing the very best that we can for the artists."[72] Still, most of the artists were satisfied just to have the opportunity.

Mural contracts were for a fixed sum, payable in installments. The artist paid all expenses associated with the mural, including art supplies and travel to the site for study of local themes and again for the mural's installation. To save on travel expenses, some artists sought out a local wallpaper hanger to install the mural, and hired a local photographer to take a picture of the completed work, a Section requirement.

The Section paid its installments based on approval of submittals as the work progressed. First, the Section suggested preliminary black-and-white sketches. "We have found that this saves time and facilitates matters for the artist," Rowan explained to one artist. Next came a color cartoon, usually scaled at two inches per foot, and upon approval, the first payment. A second payment followed a photograph of the half-finished mural or submittal of a full-sized cartoon. Transferring the scale cartoon to a full-sized canvas wasn't easy. Artist William E. L. Bunn, commissioned for the Minden, Nebraska, post office, wrote that his "enlargement is being done in sections on tracing paper by lantern slide projection."[73]

The Section authorized final payment when a mural was completed, documented by the submittal of a photograph. The postmaster was also asked to report on the installation.

To ensure lasting quality, artists filled out a form specifying the technique and medium used, the brands of paint, and a sample of the canvas. The forms received careful scrutiny. "[T]his office does not recommend the use of cotton duck canvas," Rowan warned Eugene Trentham, who was working on the post office mural for O'Neill, Nebraska. Rowan also questioned Trentham's choice of paint, saying, "We do not wish to be arbitrary in this matter, but do want the artists to use materials which will ensure the greatest permanency."[74]

The Section issued specifications for the adhesive to install murals, and requested artists to provide cleaning specifications so the mural would receive proper care in the future.

Although the commissions were not based on the artist's need for relief, they often went to struggling artists. Since artists bore the upfront costs, they often needed funds to accomplish the final mural — and Washington bureaucracy frequently caused delays in payment. Four months after Kenneth Evett completed a mural for the post office in Caldwell, Kansas, he wrote to Rowan: "[W]e're down to our last ten dollars. I can't install the completed mural until the money arrives."[75]

While working on his subsequent post office mural for Pawnee City, Nebraska, Evett was forced time and again to send letters to Rowan asking the status of his payments. "[T]his delay is demoralizing — this particular delay involves buying food and coal."[76] In another plea Evett solicited artist Carl Eric Linden to write to Rowan:

> [Evett] came to me this morning with a sad tale of waiting for his check from your office. He is down to his last dollar and has a wife and child to support. Could anything be done to *advance* or *hasten* some payment on his work ... and save him from despair and running around trying to borrow a few dollars to keep him and his family alive?

Evett wrote a strong and even more desperate letter to Rowan, saying, "The delay in getting a voucher has left me high and dry financially, behind in my rent, down to my last ten dollars and all the rest of it ... I'm in a very difficult spot and am getting damned tired of going to the mailbox day after day to find no voucher or contract, no word about the cartoon."[77]

The Section encouraged artists to visit the locale and consult with the postmaster and local people on the subject matter. Some skipped the visit to save on travel expenses, but most valued the experience and tried to satisfy the public. Even so, murals were not always favorably received despite a conscientious effort by the artist. But Bruce noted that "the occasional differences of opinion on work produced are in this sense healthy."[78]

When Archie Musick took the mural study he had painted for Greybull, Wyoming — that of cattle being loaded into a railroad car — to Red Cloud, Nebraska, he learned that local residents preferred the town's namesake, Chief Red Cloud, a subject to which he vehemently objected. However, Rowan conceded to the town's wishes and commissioned Musick to paint two other murals for the post office, one including the chief.

But despite the shortcomings the project proved its merits. "I am more and more convinced," Rowan boasted in a letter, "that one of the things our program is doing for the American artist is introducing America to the artist and thereby making the artist's efforts more meaningful to the public by this new understanding and appreciation." Bruce said that a "double purpose . . . has been served by placing these works of art in public buildings. They have added interest to the buildings and have valuably increased the fame of the artists who made them." And as artist Eugene Trentham recalled, "It has become increasingly clear to me and to all artists that while talent may flower in an Ivory Tower of isolation and poverty, it flowers considerably faster in the soil of Government patronage. At last the artist knows that he is not working for himself or a small coterie of admirers but for the people of America."[79]

The 48 States Competition

". . . mural America . . ."

The Section's most ambitious public relations effort was the "48 States Competition" of 1939. Open to all American artists, it solicited entries for one small post office in each state. The jury of distinguished artists included Maurice Stern, Henry Varnum Poor, and Edgar Miller. *Life* magazine ran photos of the winning entries in an article subtitled, "This is Mural America for Rural Americans." The author wrote, "As mural sketches, these are interesting not only in themselves but also as barometers by which everyday art taste of rural America may be judged . . . they represent in most cases the collective taste of the citizens of the community, together with the individual taste of the artist . . . Apparently rural Americans are artistic 'stay-at-homes,' with a preference for paintings that reproduce experiences and scenes and parts of history with which they are familiar."[80]

The competition's parameters recommended designs reflecting the locality, and urged artists to visit the specific post office where the mural study was intended. However, the competition resulted in something of a checkerboard game as mural studies entered for one state were sometimes selected for a post office in another state, often reflecting a topic not characteristic of the community. One Missouri artist submitted nine entries, only to be considered for a mural in a state he had not entered. Another traveled extensively to locales selected in the competition, only to win a commission for a mural in a state he had not visited. *Life* reported that "some citizens have since objected to the mural proposed for their post office and in some cases the subject is being redesigned to suit their taste."[81]

Similar scenarios played out in Nebraska. For example, Philip von Saltza's mural for the Schuyler post office was originally entered for Safford, Arizona. The Safford competition was a fruitful one — of its fifty-eight entries, three designs went to other states.[82] Archie Musick's entry for Greybull, Wyoming, went to Red Cloud, Nebraska.

In all, the competition netted 1,475 entries, resulting in an extra twenty-six post office commissions besides the original forty-eight, plus favorable nationwide publicity thanks to *Life*.[83] However, many people still considered art a luxury, and the program was viewed with less and less favor in Washington. Soon other factors would come into play and signal the end of the program.

The Final Years

"... the world going afoul ..."

The Section became a permanent part of the Treasury Department in October 1938, the fourth anniversary of its inception. Secretary Morgenthau approved the departmental order, which stated that the "leading authorities in painting and sculpture" considered the program to be meeting its objectives, and that it had "proved to be a great material and spiritual enrichment to this country."[84] But it was a short-lived coup for the newly renamed Section of Fine Arts. The next year an executive branch reorganization placed the Treasury's entire building program under the new Federal Works Agency. With that, Morgenthau's executive order was invalidated, making the program's future insecure.

By 1940 World War II was underway and the United States, while still at peace, was scaling up its military preparedness. Edward Bruce wrote to the artist who was working on a post office mural in Crawford, Nebraska:

> There is bound to be a feeling with the immense armament programs that this is no time to be spending money on art and my real hope is that we can succeed in my main theme these days that with everything in the world going afoul that we can at least keep one fine thing going and something at the end of this wretched business which we can point to with pride as being a distinguished and important achievement."[85]

In January 1941 President Roosevelt's budget called for elimination of nondefense projects. Plans for new post offices were shelved. With the country's entry into the war in December of that year, the Section began to wind down. Explaining the resulting delays in payments to artists, Rowan blamed "pressure of work in the office and a reduced staff."[86]

The war also called upon young artists such as Edward Chavez, who received a draft notice while working on his commission for the Geneva, Nebraska, post office. He contacted Rowan, who helped him get a temporary deferment so he could finish the mural. Artist Kenneth Evett inquired of Rowan if the Section was making any more commissions, saying, "I'd be grateful for one more before the Army takes me." Rowan replied that commissions "have been exhausted with the exception of a few authorizations which have been held for competition. It is our thought, however, that we would not be doing a service by announcing such competitions at this time."[87]

The Section issued its final report in 1943. In less than a decade it had commissioned more than 1,100 post office murals. Some additional murals were completed as late as 1949 under the newly organized Public Building Service.[88]

The federal art programs produced lasting benefits. As *Time* magazine predicted in 1936: "A century hence students of U.S. art in the early 1930s will probably write in their notebooks two facts: (1) It was largely a mural art; (2) It was a State-inspired art, born of the Depression, fostered by the New Deal."[89]

A Folio of Nebraska Post Office Murals

The Nebraska post office murals represent an excellent cross section of the artistic talent, subject matter, and standards set by the Section. All of the murals are still in their original settings, and all but one of the twelve buildings still serve as post offices, the exception being the Valentine building that now serves as an educational service unit for the county. The buildings remain in public ownership and are accessible to those who wish to admire the murals. All are listed in the National Register of Historic Places for their artistic merit. Because Nebraska received only smaller classifications of post offices, the Section held no competitions but selected artists based on recognized ability, most often from submissions for major commissions.

As with the Section's murals nationally, the American Scene was the predominant style in Nebraska. Both the artists and the Section avoided Social Realism; scenes of listless men in breadlines or drought-stricken farmers or foreclosure sales will not be found on Nebraska's post office walls. Instead, murals focused on people and their locales, providing a sense of hopefulness, and to most, a familiarity by depicting local subjects.

The most popular were those recalling local history. Six of the Nebraska murals depict historical themes. Today's historians may critique their accuracy, but the murals stand as products of their time, reflecting historical interpretations — and sometimes stereo-types — common in that period.

The murals show that relative newcomers to the art scene, including women and minorities, had a chance to be recognized by the Section. Women painted four of the twelve murals: those in Hebron, Valentine, Auburn, and Albion. Edward Chavez, a Mexican American artist born in New Mexico, received the commission for the Geneva post office. Many of the Nebraska muralists had little previous public exposure; Ethel Magafan, for example, was only twenty-one years old when she was commissioned for the mural in Auburn.

The Colorado Springs Fine Arts Center and the Western School of Regionalism

Students and faculty, including Frank Mechau, Edward Chavez, and the Magafan twins enjoy an outing at the Redstone Inn at Redstone, Colorado, c. 1938.

Most of the Nebraska post office murals reflect the influence of the Colorado Springs Fine Arts Center. Seven of the muralists were associated with the center, formerly known as the Broadmoor Art Academy.

The center had been under the leadership of Boardman Robinson, who came to Broadmoor as an instructor in 1930 and rose to the directorship, serving until 1947. A noted muralist, he had painted critically acclaimed private commissions for the Kaufman department store in Pittsburgh and the RKO Building at Rockefeller Center in New York City. Later, his Section commission for the Department of Justice Building in Washington, D.C., would likewise be highly regarded.

The school's other prominent instructors included Peppino Mangravite and Henry Varnum Poor, who also served a brief term as acting director. Even George Biddle, who brought the idea of public art to President Roosevelt's attention, taught a short term at the center in 1936–37.[1] Students and instructors of the Colorado center found work under the Public Works

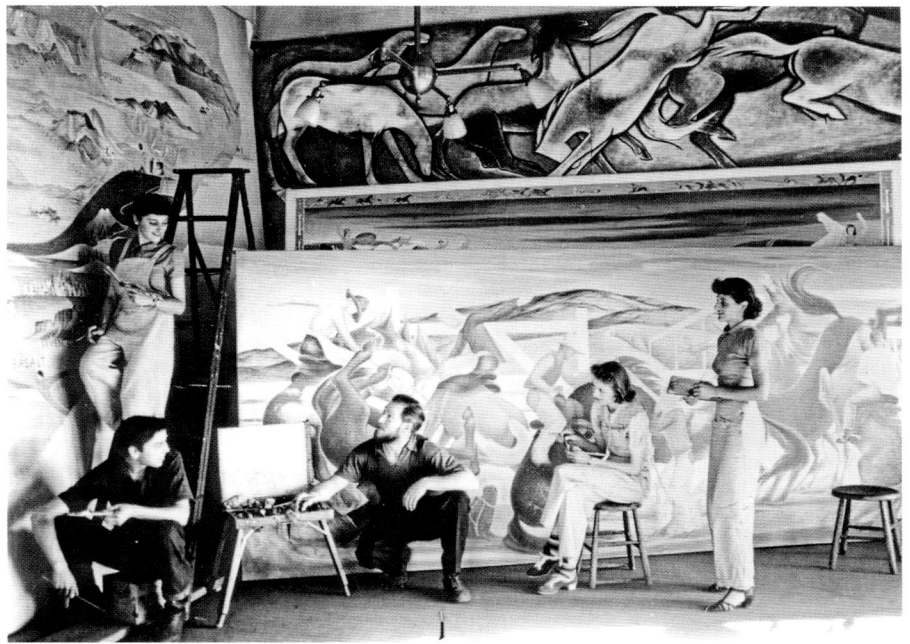

Left to right. Jenne Magafan (*on ladder*), Edward Chavez (*below*), Frank Mechau, Polly Duncan, and Ethel Magafan in Mechau's Redstone, Colorado, studio.

of Art Project, the WPA's Federal Art Project, and Treasury Relief Art Project, as well as receiving Section post office commissions.

Offering a range of arts programs, including music and theater departments, the Colorado Springs Fine Arts Center gained a national reputation — so much so that *Time* magazine referred to Colorado Springs as the "Boston of the West" upon the 1936 opening of the center's monumental new building.[2] Indeed, the opening featured a performance by dancer and choreographer Martha Graham, while sculptor Alexander Calder designed art mobiles for a stage set. Frank Mechau painted a fresco for the garden court, and Frank Lloyd Wright lectured at one of the school's conferences.

"This was my first contact with the big world of art and it was very exhilarating," recalled Kenneth Evett, who came as an assistant to Boardman Robinson in 1936. "My colleagues and assistants, the other young painters who were there[,] engaged in this activity with a real sense of purpose." A sense of camaraderie was enhanced as students and instructors participated in talent shows, art auctions, balls, outings, picnics, softball games, and swimming, and even used each other as models to save money.[3]

Frank Mechau, who served on the faculty in 1937–38, became the most prominent of the young artists associated with the Colorado Springs Fine Arts Center. He encouraged his students to paint what was around them, subjects with which they were familiar, applying boldness of line, color, and form. Together, he and his students are noted for introducing a Western school of regionalism. Three of his most gifted young students were twin sisters Jenne and Ethel Magafan, and Edward Chavez, all of whom went on to paint Nebraska post office murals.

Jenne Magafan (1916–52) | *Winter in Nebraska*

1939, OIL ON CANVAS

Jenne Magafan selected a local agricultural theme, an excellent example of the American Scene. Dominated by hues of gray, the mural evokes a cold winter evening, reading from left to right, with the farmer placed in the foreground, herding his cows toward the barn in the immediate background. In the distance is a snow-covered landscape with contours of corn rows. Blustery clouds fill the sky, and the image is framed on both sides with barren trees. Magafan prepared a mixture of varnish crystals, turpentine, and beeswax to give it a matte finish.

The Section invited Magafan to submit designs for the Albion post office based on her previous work. After traveling to the area, she submitted two subjects, one of pioneers building a sod house and another of a Nebraska landscape in winter. The Section selected the winter scene, with Rowan writing that "this possesses an extremely handsome rhythm which was not lost on us." But when Magafan submitted her two-inch-scale color sketch, Rowan, in a typical critique, raised the question of the left side of the barn, which "does not convincingly take its place in space. It seems to come up into the middle distance from the foreground . . . . The general color, however, of the design and its various elements is most commendable."[4] After Magafan submitted a photograph of her full-sized

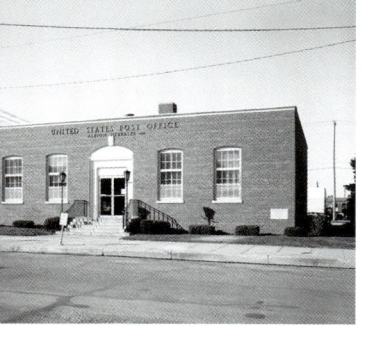

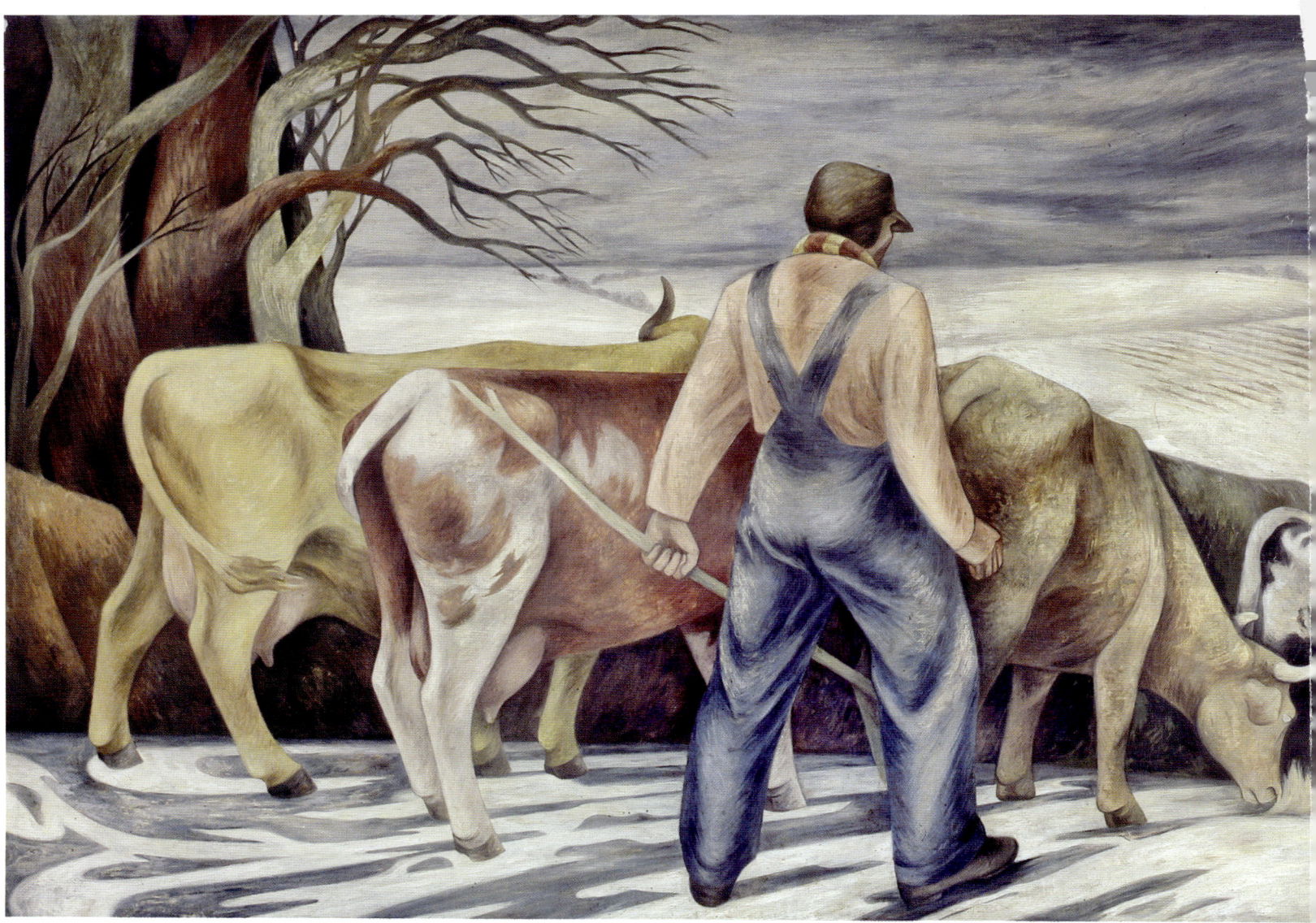

cartoon, Rowan authorized her to proceed and released the second installment of the $670 contract. However, he suggested that she "check the drawing of the hind quarters of the second cow to the left. The leg seems somewhat heavy in the middle." After seeing a photograph of the completed work, Rowan praised it as "quite handsome in quality."[5]

Accompanied by her twin sister Ethel and fellow student (and future husband) Edward Chavez, Magafan installed the mural during a "very swell trip" to Nebraska. She was pleased with the community's response. "They were terribly interested and enthusiastic with the idea of having a mural in their town. There was also the feeling that it was a great privilege that Washington should choose to give them a mural." But after a picture of her work was reproduced in the *Omaha World-Herald* it spurred an editorial attributed to "Cactus Ike," an anonymous and folksy writer: "I figure this no doubt is a right nice bit of art . . . and she sure made it look right chilly with the sky full of dark, blusterin' clouds and the wind blowin' the tree branches around and the ground covered with snow . . . but the young lady evidently overlooked the fact that out here in Nebraska when it really gets cold the farmers keep on bein' farmers by wearing more than a pair of suspenders over their shoulders." According to the Albion postmaster, local residents shared Cactus Ike's opinion.[6] The Section, however, was so pleased with the mural that they asked Magafan if they could use her cartoon for an exhibition of mural studies at the Corcoran Gallery in Washington, D.C.

JENNE AND ETHEL MAGAFAN were first exposed to art by an inspiring teacher, Miss Helen Perry, at Denver's East High School. She was so impressed with their talent that she paid the twins' tuition to study with Frank Mechau at his School of Modern Art in Denver. In 1936 Jenne and her sister followed Mechau to the Colorado Springs Fine Arts Center when he became an instructor there.[7] The sisters assisted with his mural for the Colorado Springs post office, among others. Jenne also trained under Peppino Mangravite while at the center.

Magafan's murals included a collaboration with Edward Chavez for the Glenwood Springs, Colorado, post office, a TRAP commission done under the supervision of Frank Mechau. For the Section, she painted post office murals in Anson, Texas, and Helper,

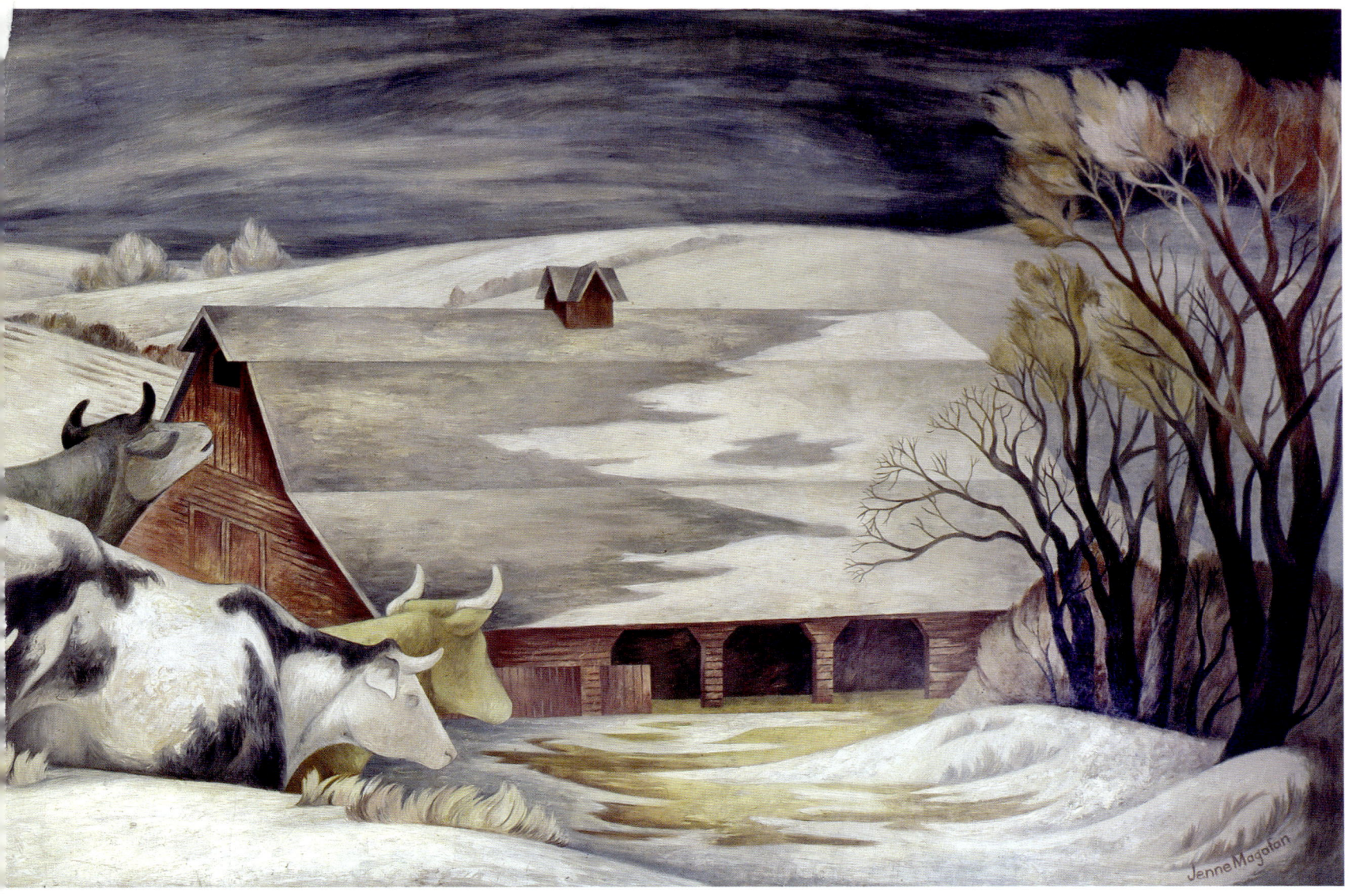

PLATE 1

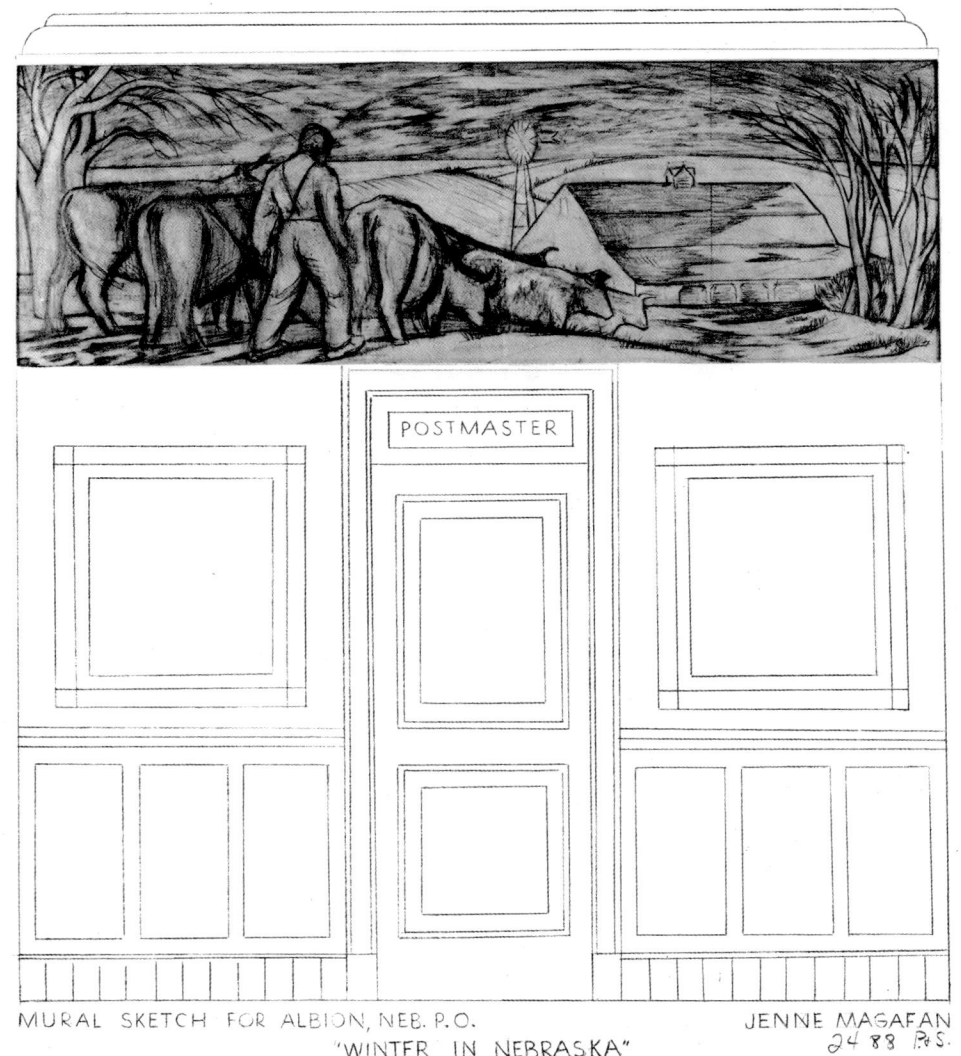

MURAL SKETCH FOR ALBION, NEB. P.O.　　　　　　JENNE MAGAFAN
'WINTER IN NEBRASKA'　　　　　　　　　　　　24 88 Pos.

Jenne Magafan's sketch for the Albion mural.

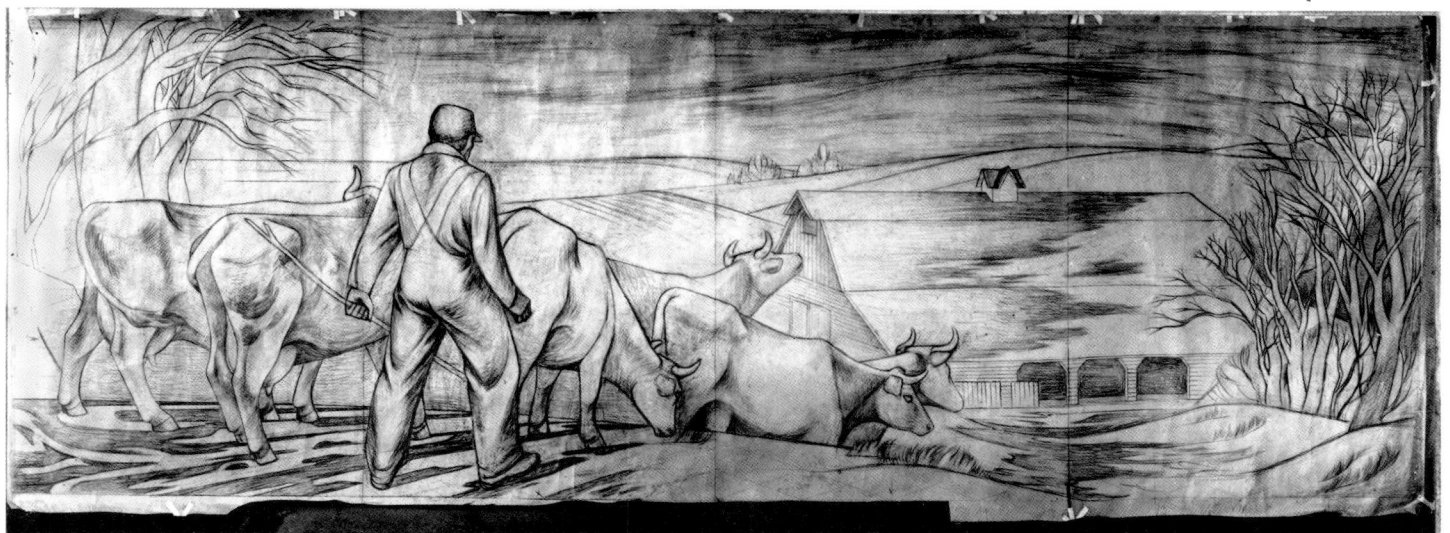

Full-sized cartoon of the Albion mural. Rowan suggested that Magafan "check the drawing of the hind quarters of the second cow to the left."

Utah — the latter being awarded under the 48 States Competition. In all, the Magafan twins completed seven post office murals for the Section and collaborated on another mural for the Social Security Building in Washington, D.C. She settled in Woodstock, New York, where she shared her artistic endeavors with husband Edward Chavez. The twins traveled the Mediterranean in 1951–52 after Ethel Magafan and Edward Chavez received Fulbright scholarships to study overseas. Less than a week after their return, Jenne died suddenly of a cerebral hemorrhage at the age of thirty-six.

Ethel Magafan (1916–93) | *Threshing*

1938, TEMPERA AND OIL ON CANVAS

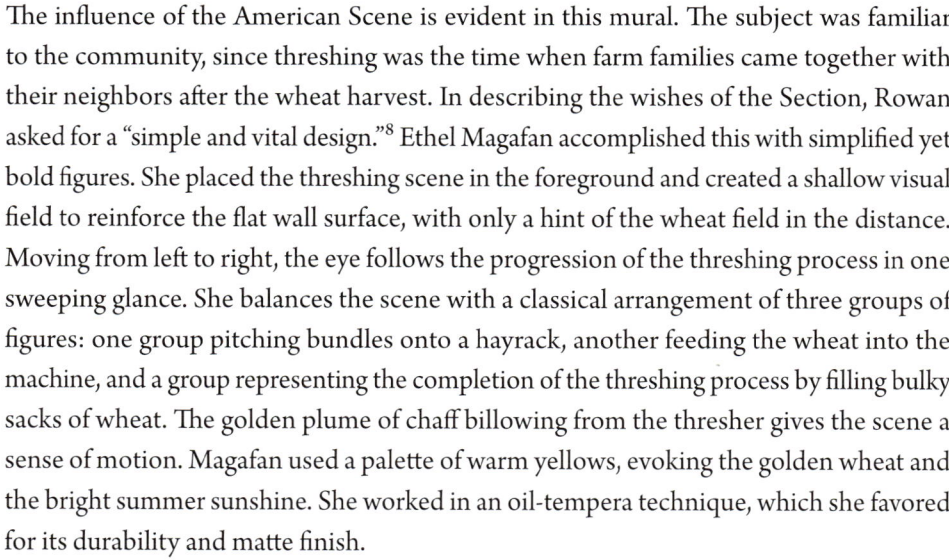

The influence of the American Scene is evident in this mural. The subject was familiar to the community, since threshing was the time when farm families came together with their neighbors after the wheat harvest. In describing the wishes of the Section, Rowan asked for a "simple and vital design."[8] Ethel Magafan accomplished this with simplified yet bold figures. She placed the threshing scene in the foreground and created a shallow visual field to reinforce the flat wall surface, with only a hint of the wheat field in the distance. Moving from left to right, the eye follows the progression of the threshing process in one sweeping glance. She balances the scene with a classical arrangement of three groups of figures: one group pitching bundles onto a hayrack, another feeding the wheat into the machine, and a group representing the completion of the threshing process by filling bulky sacks of wheat. The golden plume of chaff billowing from the thresher gives the scene a sense of motion. Magafan used a palette of warm yellows, evoking the golden wheat and the bright summer sunshine. She worked in an oil-tempera technique, which she favored for its durability and matte finish.

Magafan's first opportunity for a post office commission resulted from her entry into a juried competition for the Fort Scott, Kansas, post office. The Section thought highly of

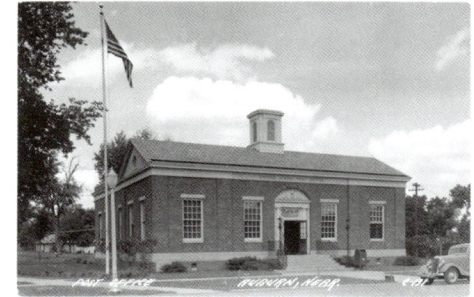

her submittal — a historical portrayal of the bloody 1863 massacre at Lawrence, Kansas, by pro-slavery raiders — but the local jury did not. They found the subject controversial and highly objectionable. In such cases, the Section usually bowed to local comment, and did so in this case.

"I was rather naïve," Magafan later said of the experience.[9] Nevertheless, she received the $620 Auburn commission on a noncompetitive basis, her first of many murals for the Section. From her Fort Scott experience she apparently learned to "paint Section," and with the Auburn mural met the expectations both of project administrators and the public.

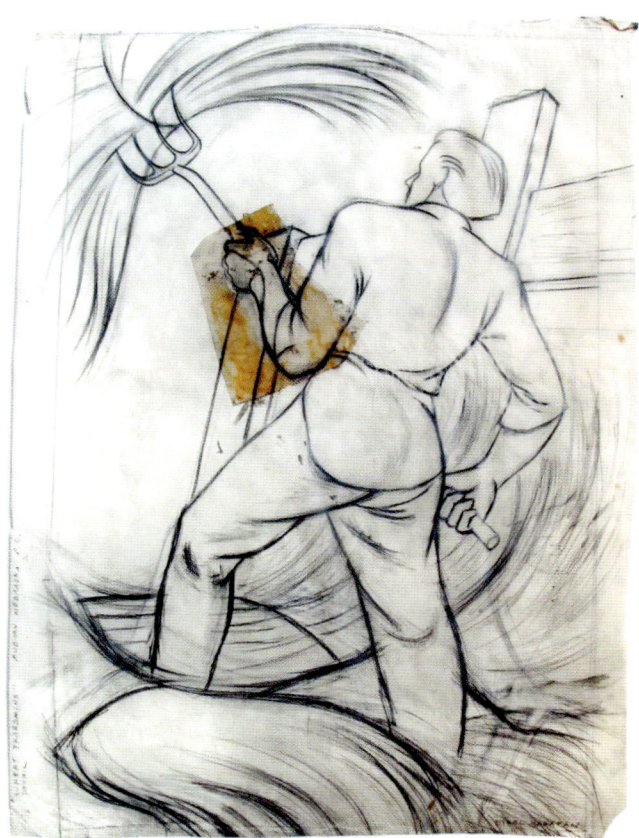

A detail study of one of the figures in Ethel Magafan's *Threshing*.

Magafan traveled to Auburn, where she met the postmaster and sketched local landscapes. She submitted two pencil sketches, one showing a local landscape and the other a scene of threshing wheat, along with a color sketch of a Colorado landscape as an example of her use of color. When the threshing scene was selected, Rowan forwarded high praise from members of the Section and the supervising architect: "The colored landscape was regarded as quite delightful and I trust that a similar palette and approach may be used in the threshing scene."[10]

After Magafan showed her color sketch of the proposed mural to Peppino Mangravite, then serving as art director and instructor at the Colorado Springs Fine Arts Center, she wrote to the Section that he wanted them to know that "he almost danced with joy when he saw it." Rowan replied that the Section shared his enthusiasm. The piece was a "very fine accomplishment," he wrote. Unlike the "correspondence course" with other artists, Rowan offered no criticism or suggestions for improvement throughout the creation of her work. He simply wrote, "I trust that it will be possible for you to retain in the finished work, all of the charm of characterization that so enhanced the color sketch."[11]

The completed mural was well received by the postmaster, the local newspaper, and a ladies' art class. The art class, which previously expressed their preference for a topic of local history, indicated that a "better subject could not have been choosed [*sic*] as the old threshing machine is

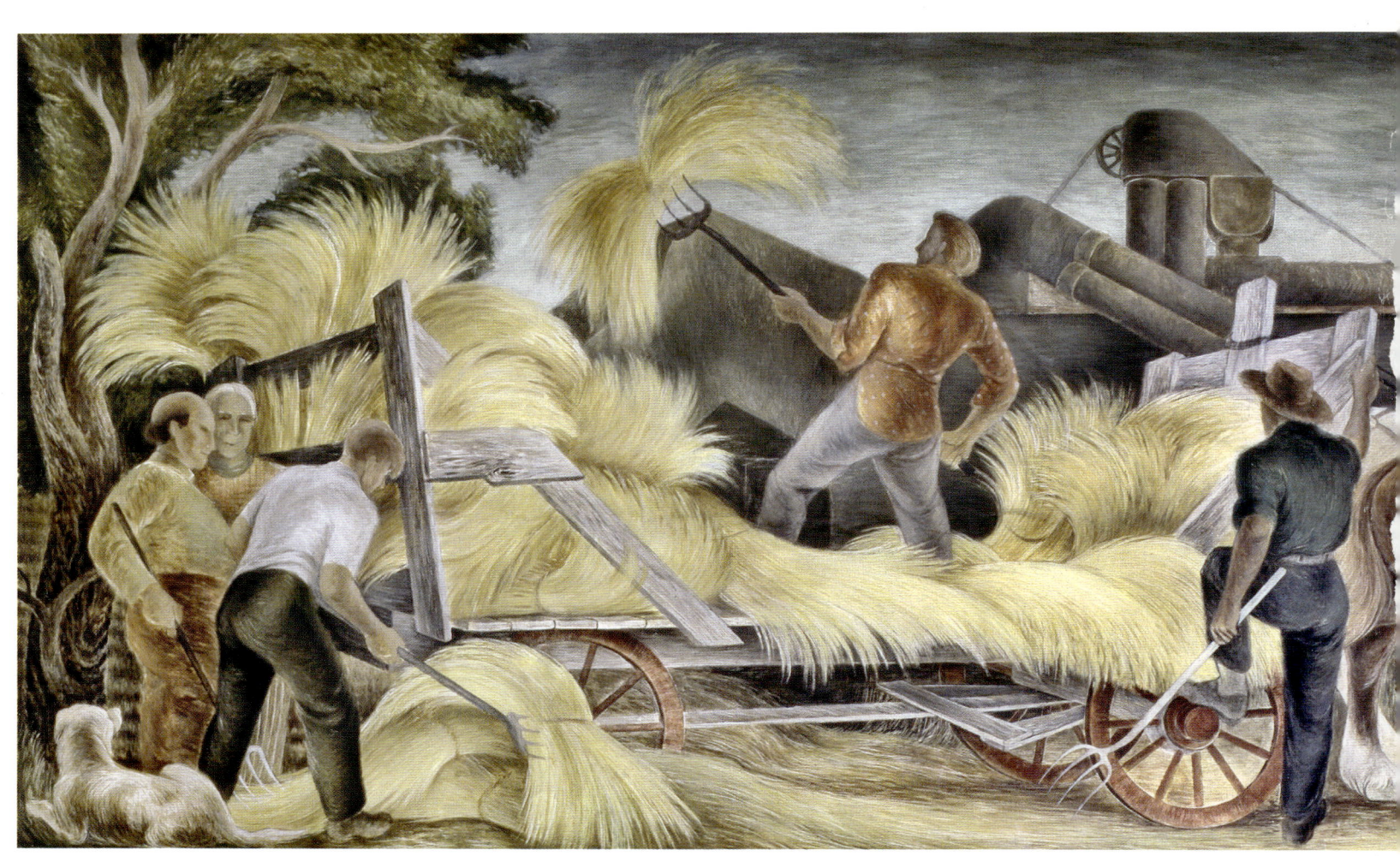

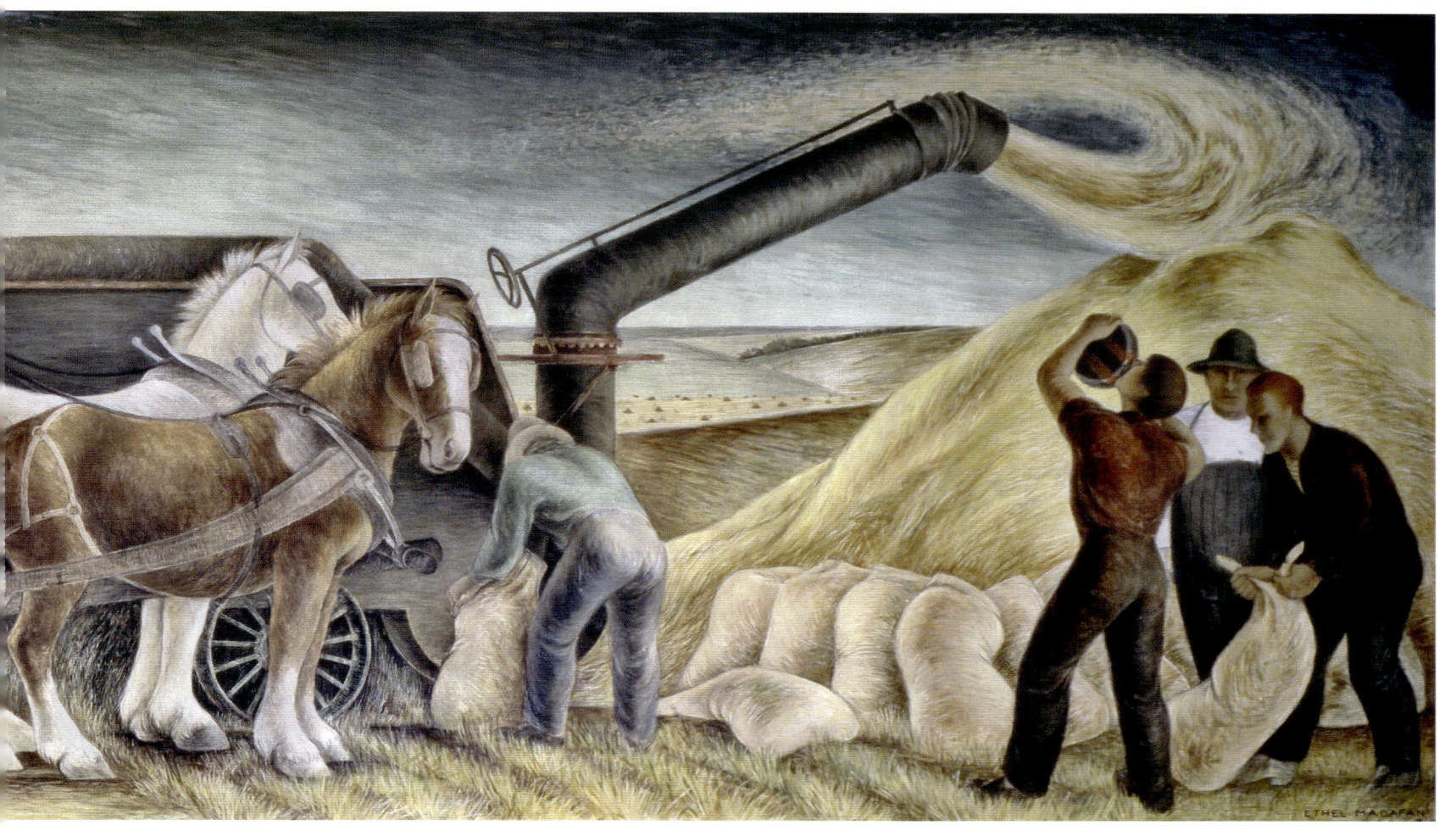

PLATE 2

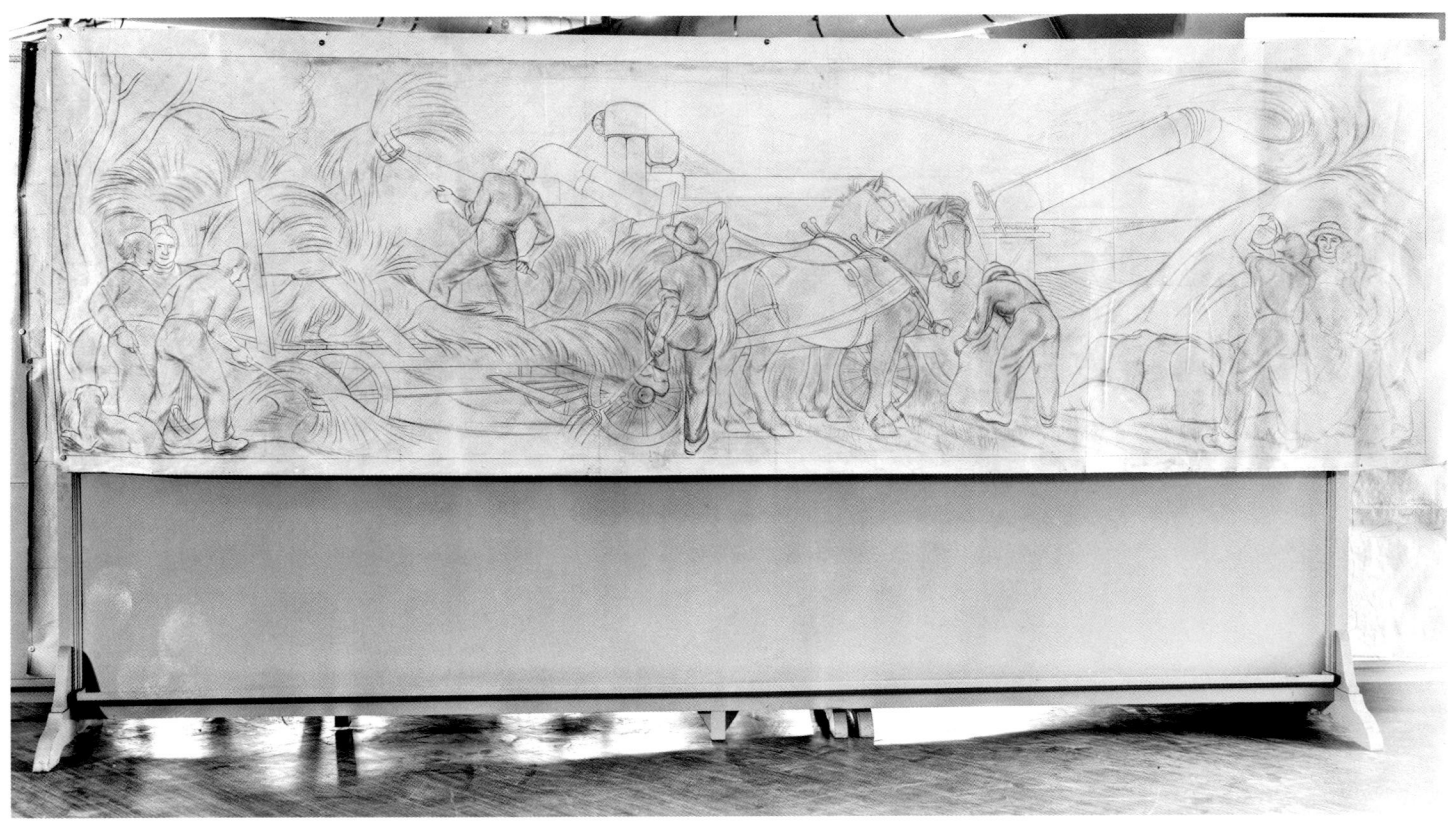

Full-size cartoon of *Threshing*.

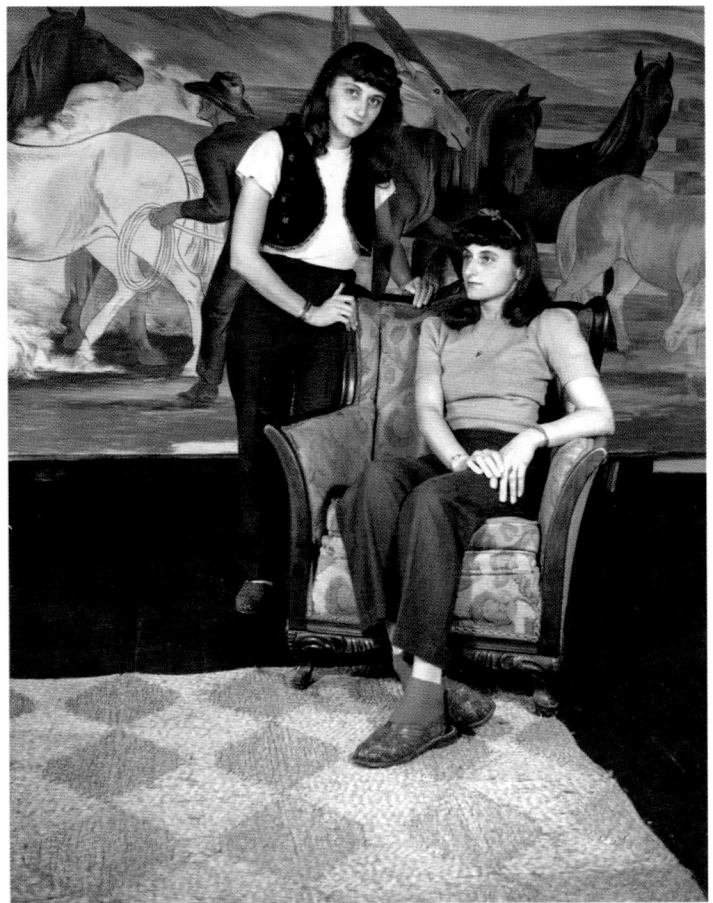

Jenne and Ethel Magafan pose before Ethel's completed mural for the South Denver Branch post office, entitled *Horse Corral* (1942).

rapidly going out of use and in side [*sic*] of another generation it will be a thing of the past and this will stand as a memory of the by gone [*sic*] days . . . [S]ome day it may be as popular as the one so recently painted by Grant Wood — *Dinner for Threshers*." Rowan agreed: "In our opinion Miss Magafan's work is in every way equal to that painting."[12]

ETHEL MAGAFAN AND HER SISTER, Jenne, attended East High School in Denver where they were classmates with Edward Chavez. They met Frank Mechau when he visited their classroom. As described in Jenne's biographical sketch on p. 38, the sisters went on to study under Mechau at his School of Modern Art in Denver, at his studio in Redstone, Colorado, and at the Colorado Springs Fine Arts Center. Ethel became a most prolific artist of post office murals, completing four for the Section, including the Wynne, Arkansas, Madill, Oklahoma, and South Denver Branch post offices.

With the discovery of Ethel's talents through the federal arts projects, she became highly recognized and was awarded mural commissions in Washington, D.C., for the Recorder of Deeds Building (1943) and the Social Security Building (1949), the latter in collaboration with her sister for the Public Building Service. She settled in Woodstock, New York, where she met her future husband, artist Bruce Currie. They were fixtures in the Woodstock art scene, though Ethel continued to be attracted to the West and made annual trips to the mountains. She won a Fulbright scholarship to study in Greece, her father's homeland, and was accompanied by Jenne and Edward Chavez on the trip in 1951–52.

Ethel had a long and distinguished career as an easel painter, exhibiting widely and winning many prestigious awards. Her painting style gradually evolved from the realistic to the semi-abstract.[13] In 1968 she was elected an academician of the National Academy of Design. She continued painting into her mid-seventies.

G. Glenn Newell (1870–1947) | *The Crossing*

1940, OIL ON CANVAS

G. Glenn Newell, commissioned for the post office in Crawford, Nebraska, selected for his subject a wagon train of pioneers, depicting what he described as "sunshine—youth—action."[14] The stream shimmers with light, shadows, and reflections as wagons prepare to cross. Silhouettes of wagons curve in the distance along a ridgeline. Storm clouds rise in the distance. At age seventy, Newell was the oldest artist to paint a Nebraska mural, and his work reflects the older, more traditional style in which he practiced.

Newell was selected for the Crawford commission based on his entry for the Poughkeepsie, New York, post office. Already known for his paintings of farm animals and pastoral landscapes, Newell had submitted a composition depicting cattle. Rowan then asked him to write to the Crawford postmaster "to see if one of your interesting compositions dealing with the subject matter of cows would not be appropriate for the decoration of his building." Newell replied favorably, and said that he was "already working on it in my 'Think Shop.'" Newell also indicated that he had previously attempted some subjects of potential local interest, such as plowing a field with oxen, or pioneers crossing the Platte River valley in covered wagons. Rowan suggested pioneers crossing the Niobrara River.[15]

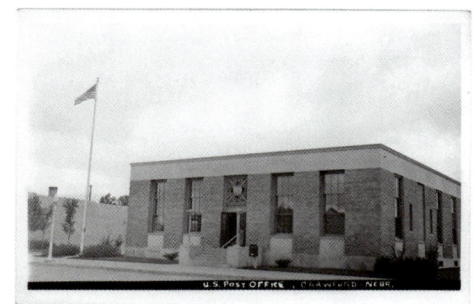

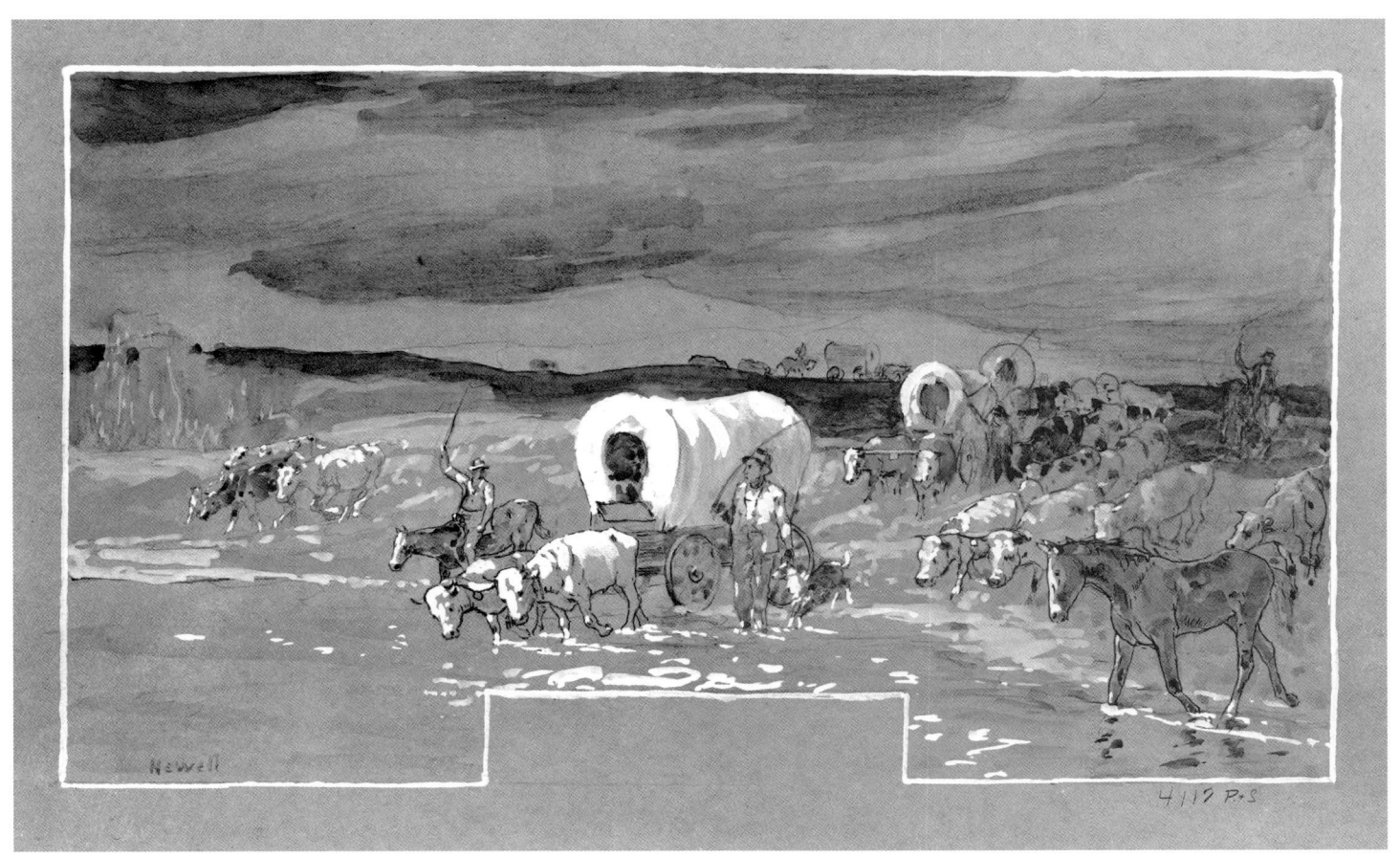

One of three of the first subjects submitted
by Newell for the Crawford post office mural.

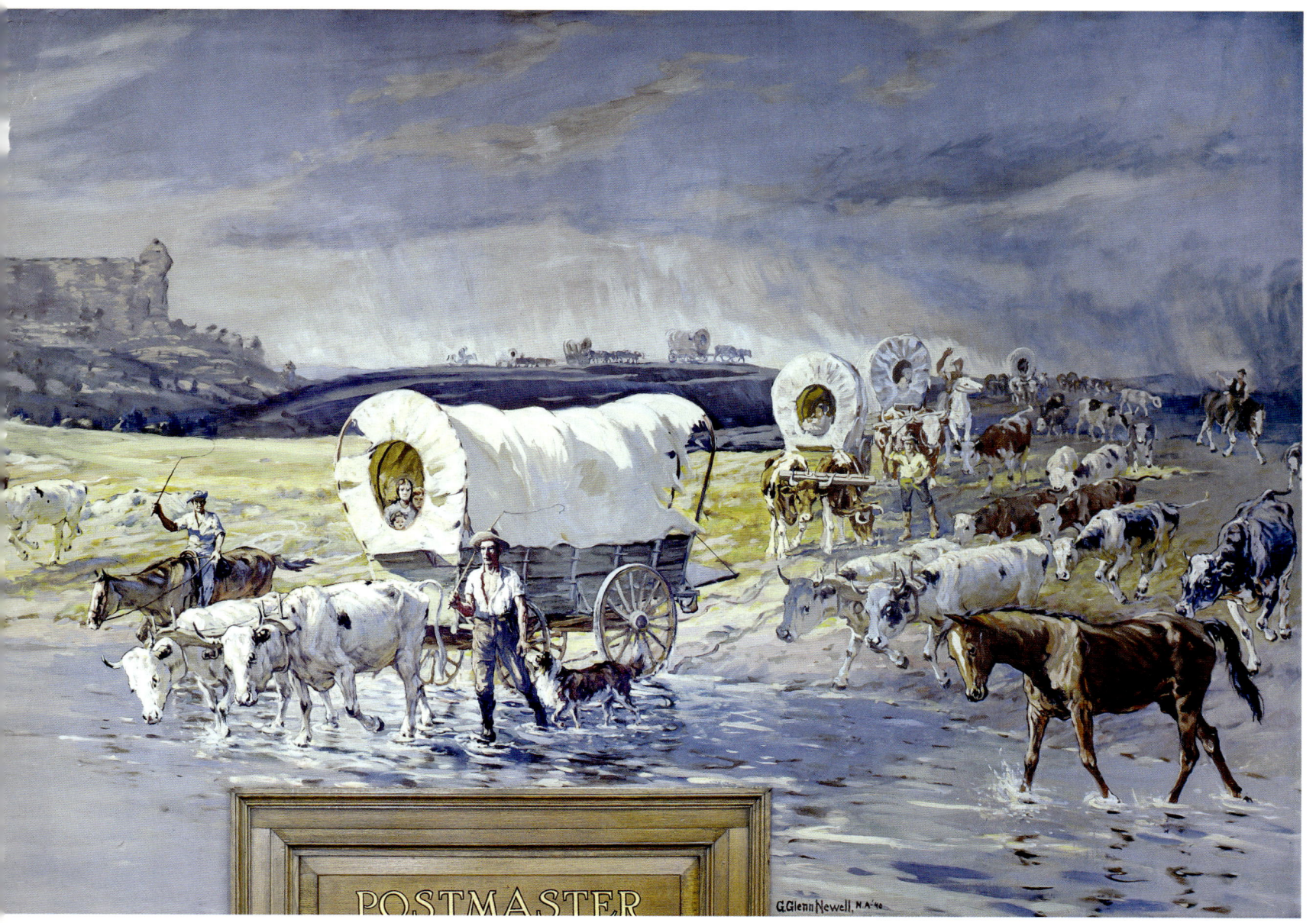

POSTMASTER

G.Glenn Newell, N.A.'40

PLATE 3

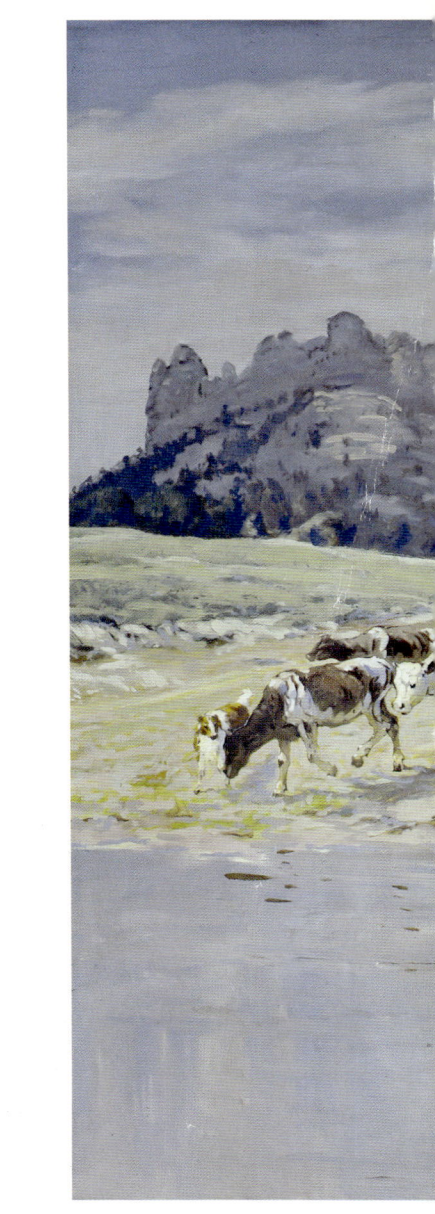

Newell entered the Section's "correspondence course" with his submittal of three subjects. The Section preferred the river crossing, with the criticism that he "check carefully the scale of the figure in front of the covered wagon as the two do not seem related."[16] He was authorized to proceed with the full-size cartoon and received the first installment of his $800 contract. To address the Section's criticism, Newell corrected the scale of the foreground figure.

Although he painted the mural in his studio without visiting the locale, Newell tried to be accurate to the local landscape. While working on the full-sized cartoon he obtained a small photograph of Crow Butte, which he selected as the backdrop. "[A] beautiful castellated formation near Crawford . . . it was just what I wanted. It gives a definite and local aspect to [the] picture." But when he submitted a photograph of his nearly completed canvas, the Section responded with more criticism. Rowan wrote "the scale of the man on the horse entering the stream, left of the wagon, has been reduced too suddenly. You will note that his head is no larger than those of the figures in middle distance [and] the horse on the right does not give the indication of walking in water."[17]

Newell complied with the "constructive suggestions," although he was hesitant to cover the horse's hooves. "I hated to cover feet (like they all do) but must sacrifice my drawing I suppose." He said of his work's complexity: "There being fifty-two figures in this composition it requires ingenuity to relate all."[18]

As the work neared completion, Newell suggested the following verse to include in the mural:

Seeking the Western sunshine,
Leaving the storms behind,
Taking sires of the future with them,
And dams of better kind.[19]

Rowan politely declined the suggestion.

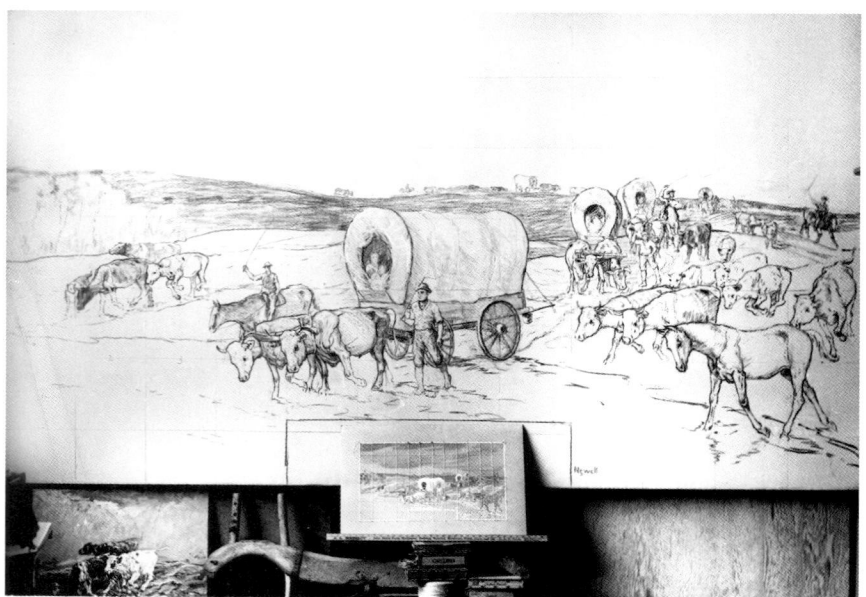

Outline drawing of the full-sized canvas. Newell used his two-inch-scale study (below canvas) in the process of enlarging the image.

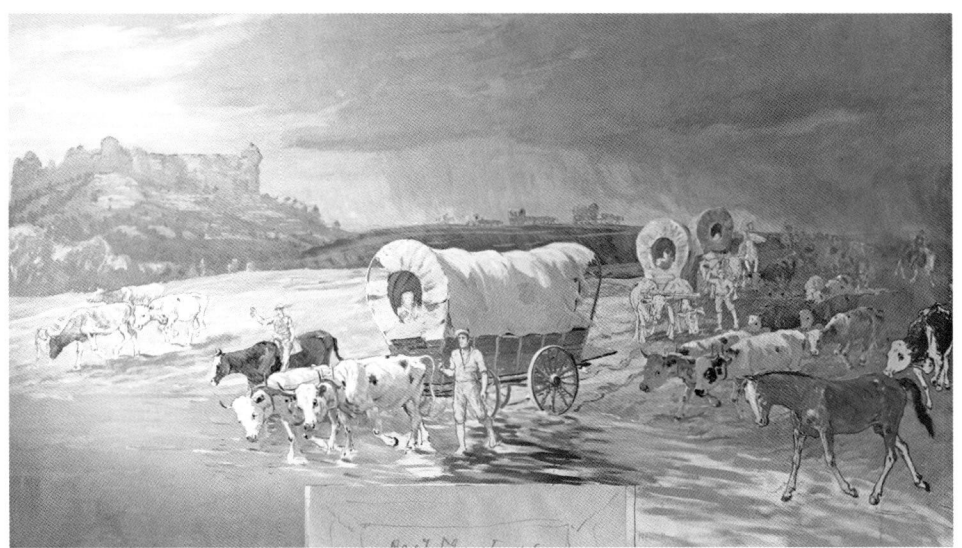

The completed mural was well received locally. The Crawford newspaper remarked, "A thing of beauty is attracting many people to the post office . . . [it] is quite appropriate to this northwestern country and will bring vivid memories to many of our pioneers." And in another article: "Mr. Newell's portrayal of this seemingly endless wagon train is naturally symbolic of the whole 'westward march of civilization.'"[20]

Final canvas for the Crawford post office. Newell would accept the Section's criticism for the horseman on the left and the horse on the right, which were changed before installation. He added Crow Butte in the background.

NEWELL WAS BORN in Michigan and studied at the National Academy of Design and Columbia University in New York City. He became something of a gentleman farmer in Dutchess County, New York, where he kept dairy cattle and was a painter of farm life. One of his paintings was displayed at the 1898 Trans-Mississippi and International Exposition in Omaha; years later another was selected for the private collection of President Roosevelt, whom he knew as a fellow resident of Dutchess County. Newell was elected an associate member of the National Academy of Design in 1918, becoming a full academician in 1937. He served as president of the Allied Artists of America from 1919 to 1926.[21] After the Crawford commission, he went on to complete another Section post office mural in Wallace, North Carolina.

Edward Chavez (1917–95) | *Building a Sod House*

1941, OIL AND TEMPERA ON CANVAS

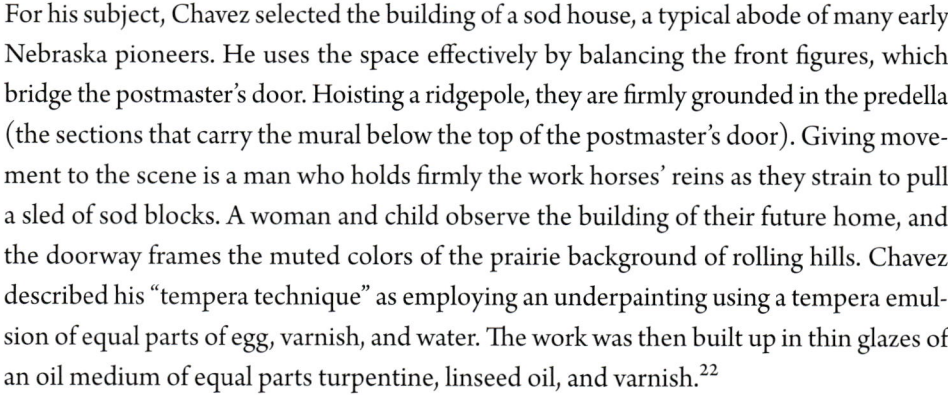

For his subject, Chavez selected the building of a sod house, a typical abode of many early Nebraska pioneers. He uses the space effectively by balancing the front figures, which bridge the postmaster's door. Hoisting a ridgepole, they are firmly grounded in the predella (the sections that carry the mural below the top of the postmaster's door). Giving movement to the scene is a man who holds firmly the work horses' reins as they strain to pull a sled of sod blocks. A woman and child observe the building of their future home, and the doorway frames the muted colors of the prairie background of rolling hills. Chavez described his "tempera technique" as employing an underpainting using a tempera emulsion of equal parts of egg, varnish, and water. The work was then built up in thin glazes of an oil medium of equal parts turpentine, linseed oil, and varnish.[22]

Chavez was selected for the Geneva post office on the basis of designs submitted for the Social Security Building in Washington, D.C. Although discouraged by not getting a commission of this prominence, he gratefully accepted the $750 job. He traveled to Geneva and consulted with the postmaster on subject matter but observed that "the community being primarily a farming community [has] no special historical incidents etc." He submitted two pencil sketches, one of a farm scene with cattle feeding at a haystack. The

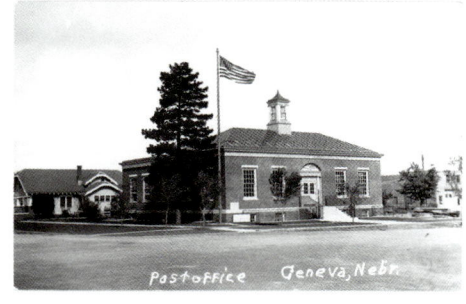

Post office Geneva, Nebr.

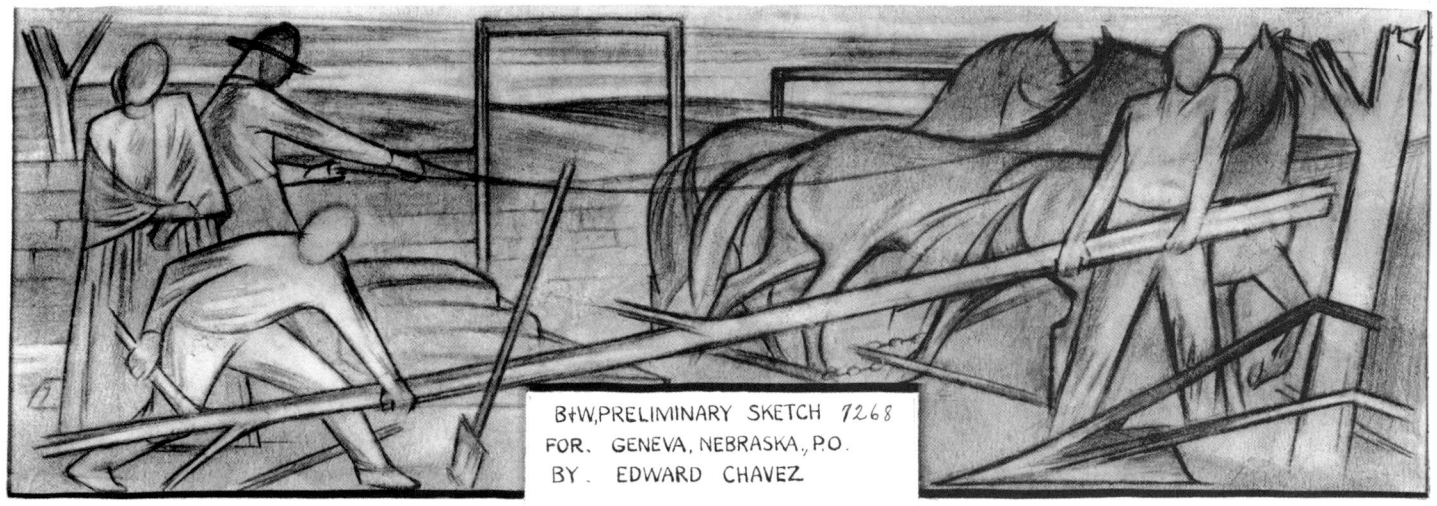

B+W, PRELIMINARY SKETCH 1268
FOR. GENEVA, NEBRASKA., P.O.
BY. EDWARD CHAVEZ

Chavez submitted a simplified version of his subject for the preliminary black-and-white sketch.

other was of pioneers building a sod house, a composition with strong outlines and few details of the figures. It had historical significance, he said, "since the 'Sod House' typifys [*sic*] the early settler on the Neb. prairie." Although it is not known to what extent Chavez studied the techniques of constructing a sod house, his depiction is quite accurate. The doors and windows are shown being framed in timber, which would carry the weight of the sod. In the foreground is a representation of the plow that broke the sod. Chavez later said, "I did extensive research on all my submissions [to the Section] for the sake of accuracy though artists did exert a certain amount of poetic license."[23]

Rowan wrote enthusiastically of the Section's approval of the sketch: "[It] seems more distinguished as a composition and equally interesting in subject matter. In fact the composition is well related to the space and I personally thought you should be congratulated on your achievement."[24]

Upon receiving the two-inch-scale color sketch Rowan asked Chavez to restudy the foreground figure to the left. "We find it a little disturbing to have the contour of an element seemingly coincide with the contour of another element; in this case the arm and the torso. Continue also to work for convincing spatial relations so that one has the feeling

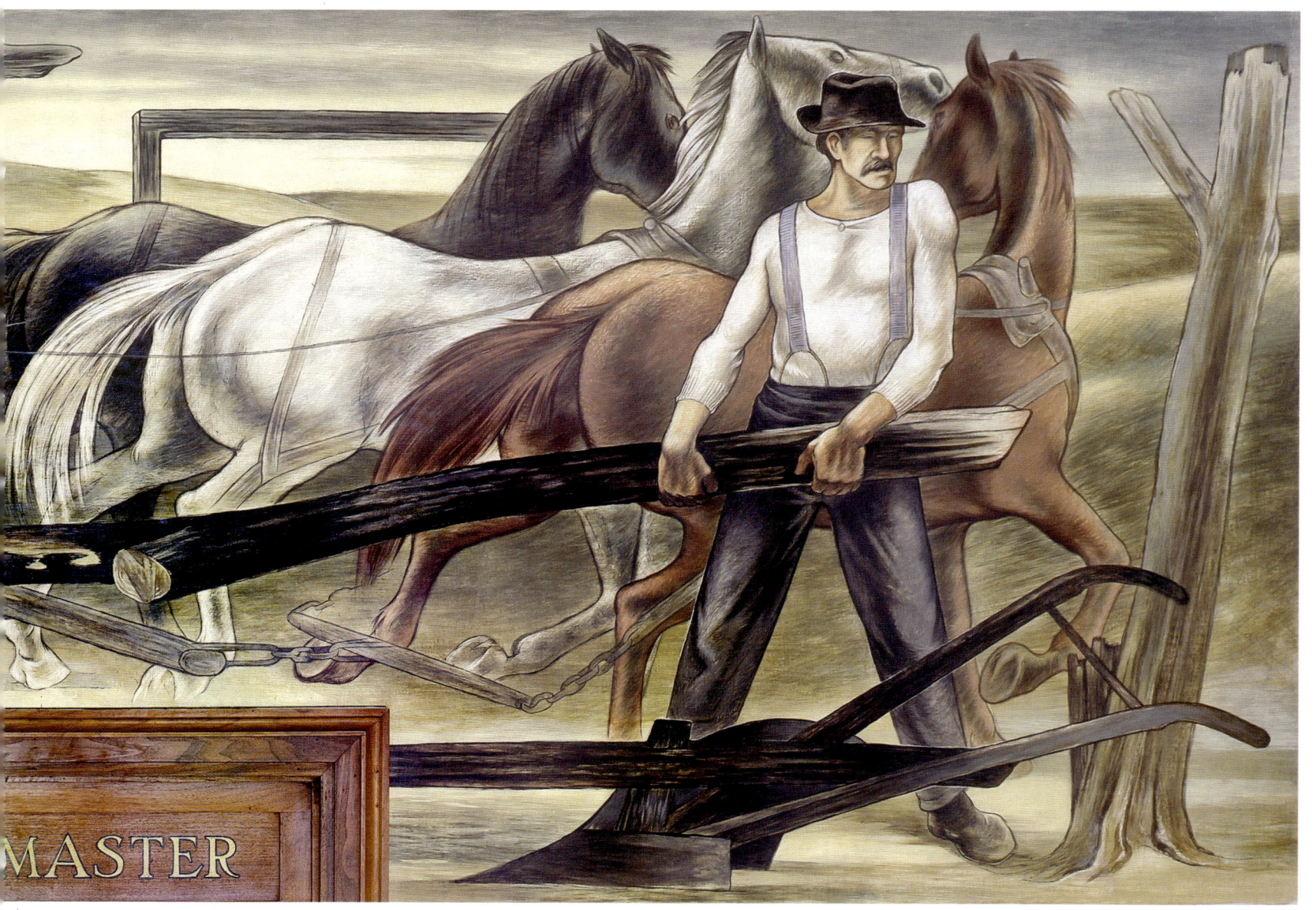

MASTER

PLATE 4

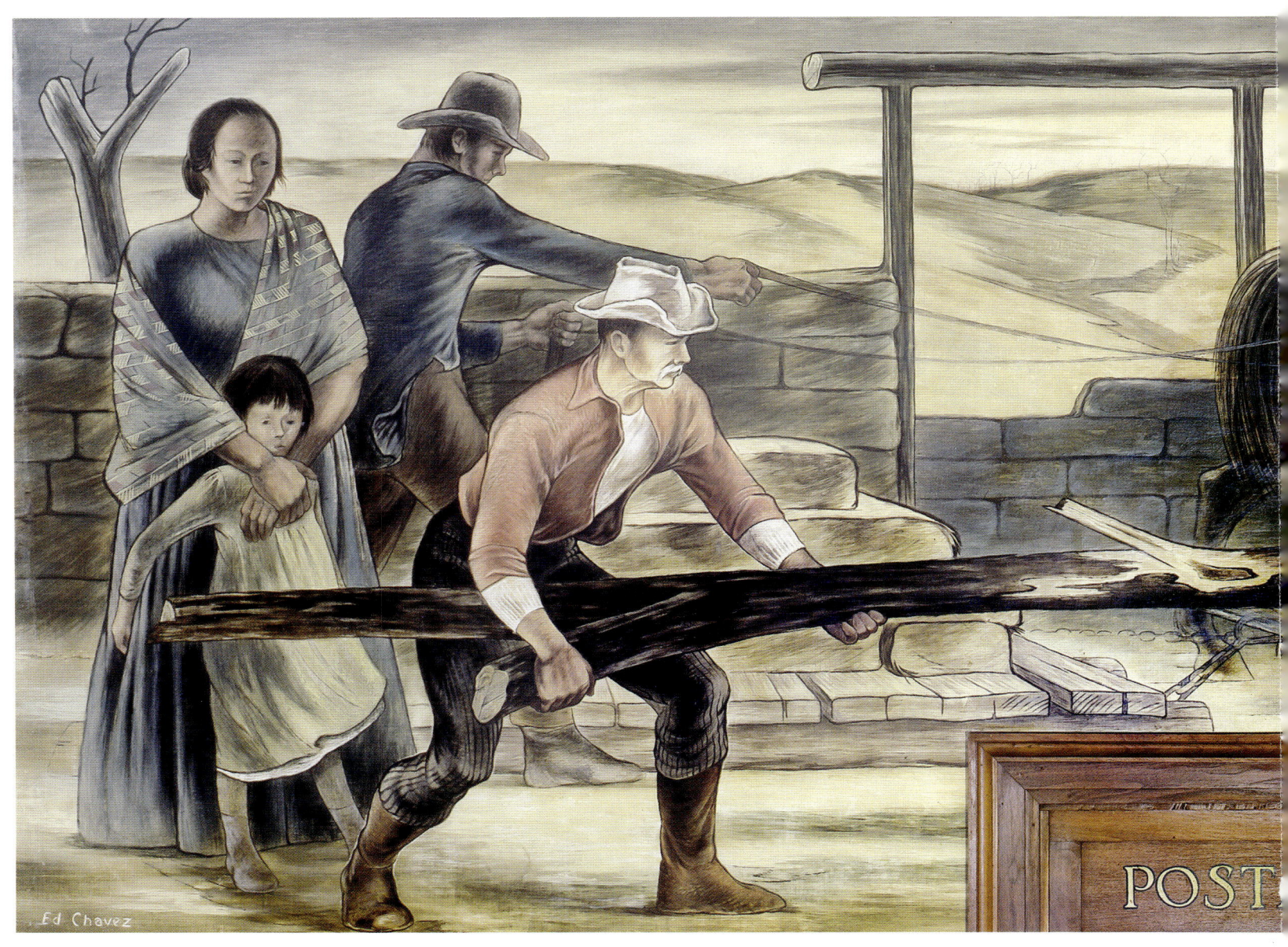

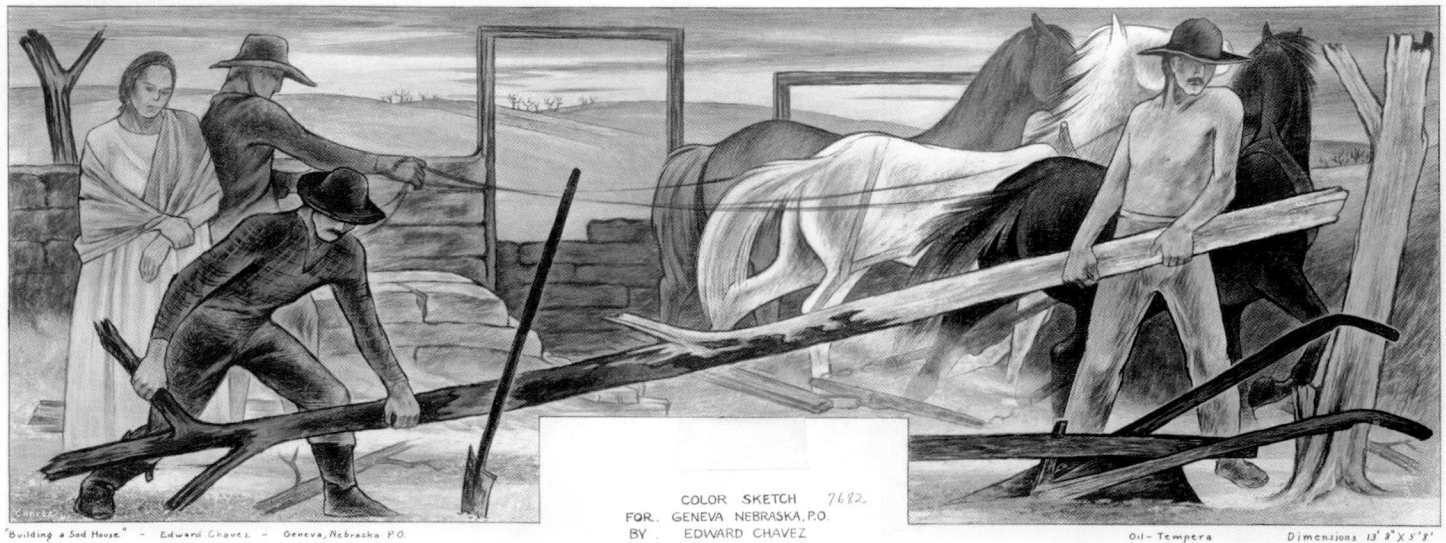

COLOR SKETCH 7682
FOR GENEVA NEBRASKA, P.O.
BY EDWARD CHAVEZ

"Building a Sod House" - Edward Chavez - Geneva, Nebraska P.O.

Oil-Tempera   Dimensions 13'3"X 5'8'

Color sketch for the Geneva mural. From a 1941 photograph.

that every section of an element introduced into the design is realized throughout."[25] But apparently satisfied with the overall composition, Rowan directed Chavez to proceed with the full-size cartoon.

The completed mural satisfied both the artist and his colleagues, the Magafan sisters: "The Twins and I thought this was a better job than the last one." He was apparently comparing it to the one he had completed for the Center, Texas, post office. Upon its completion, the Geneva post office custodian reported, "I have received from the public many favorable comments on the mural . . . as a fine addition to the decorations of the building."[26]

BORN IN NEW MEXICO, as a boy Chavez moved with his family to Colorado. Along with his classmates the Magafan twins, "an exceptional teacher" at Denver's East High School introduced him to art. In his youth he was influenced by José Clemente Orozco and David Alfaro Siqueiros, two of the muralists under the Mexican government's art project. Although Chavez considered himself self-taught, he studied at the Colorado Springs Fine Arts Center under Boardman Robinson and Peppino Mangravite. But he recognized that his principal influence was Frank Mechau, under whom he studied at the Colorado center.[27]

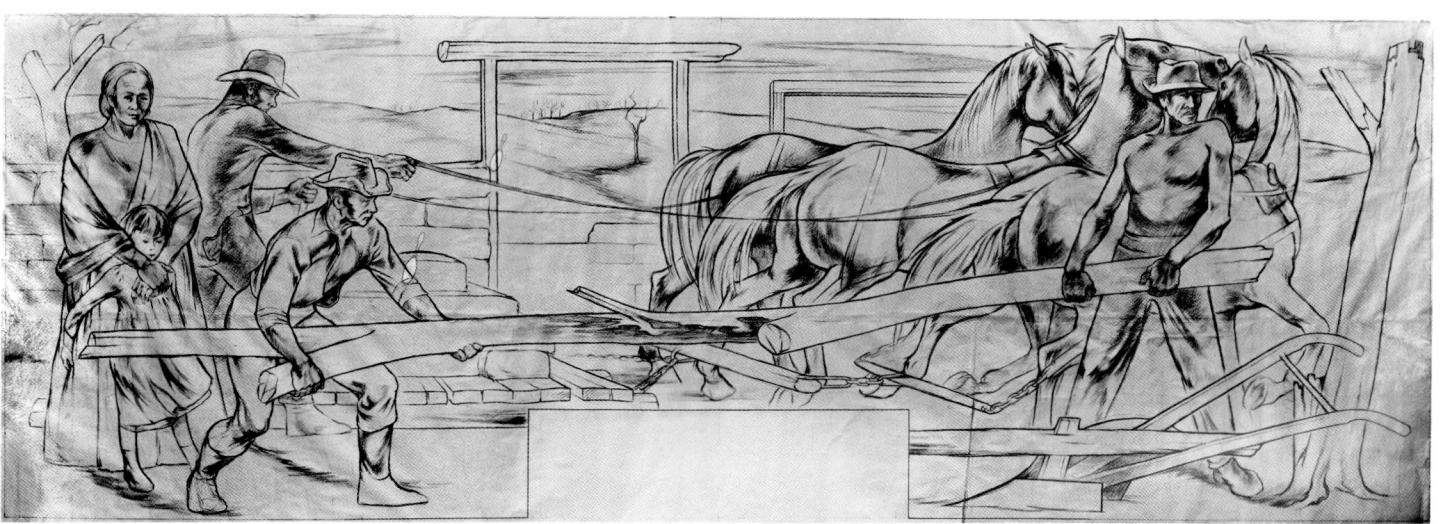

Full-size cartoon for the Geneva mural. Chavez added a child with the mother in the final version.

Chavez completed a mural for the Denver's West High School under the WPA's Fine Art Project and worked with Jenne Magafan on the Glenwood Springs, Colorado, post office mural, a commission of the Treasury Relief Art Project. The mural for the Center, Texas, post office was his only other commission from the Section. The noteworthy characteristic of the federal art projects, he said later, was "in the contact that one had with the audience for which one was painting, or in other words, there was a more direct influence between the audience and the artist."[28] During his service in World War II he continued his art, was tapped for a position with an art unit to document the war in photography and paintings, and won a *Life* magazine competition in 1942 with a watercolor of a military scene called *Convoy Practice*. After returning from service he married Jenne Magafan and settled in the art colony in Woodstock, New York. He won a Fulbright scholarship to study in Italy, a trip accompanied by the twins in 1951–52. He taught at the Art Students League in New York City and Syracuse University School of Art, among others. He remained part of the art scene in Woodstock and co-founded the Woodstock School of Art in 1968. He deviated from a regionalist style to abstraction during his life and worked in a variety of media, including painting, graphics, and sculpture.

Eldora Lorenzini (1910–93)

Stampeding Buffaloes Stopping the Train

1939, OIL ON CANVAS

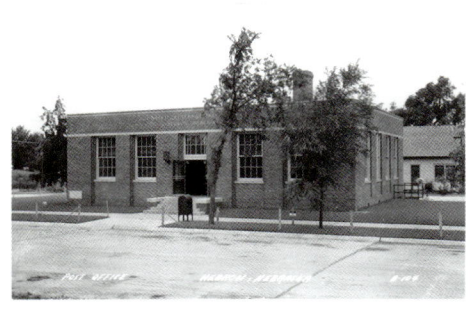

Painted in hues of brown and gold, a group of men take sport in shooting into the great buffalo herd that is stopping the train. In the background Eldora Lorenzini depicts the treeless plains under a blue-gray sky. The herd recedes into the background providing a sense of depth, while the large figures of buffalo in the foreground almost stop the herd from running off the lower canvas. Like many of the historical murals dealing with westward movement, the mural was "symbolic of the conflict in which the wilderness gives way to civilization," according to a local newspaper.[29]

Lorenzini was selected for the Hebron post office mural based on sketches she submitted for the new Department of Interior Building in Washington, D.C. She traveled to Hebron and selected a historical theme, receiving photographs and material to study for subject matter. Probably overeager for her first commission, she passed along the suggestion that she paint not only a mural above the postmaster's door, but also three murals on the screen wall above the postal clerks' service windows. Rowan cautioned her that "the amount of the reservation for this work would hardly justify you in undertaking so extensive a scheme."[30] She followed with two sketches for the space above the postmaster's door.

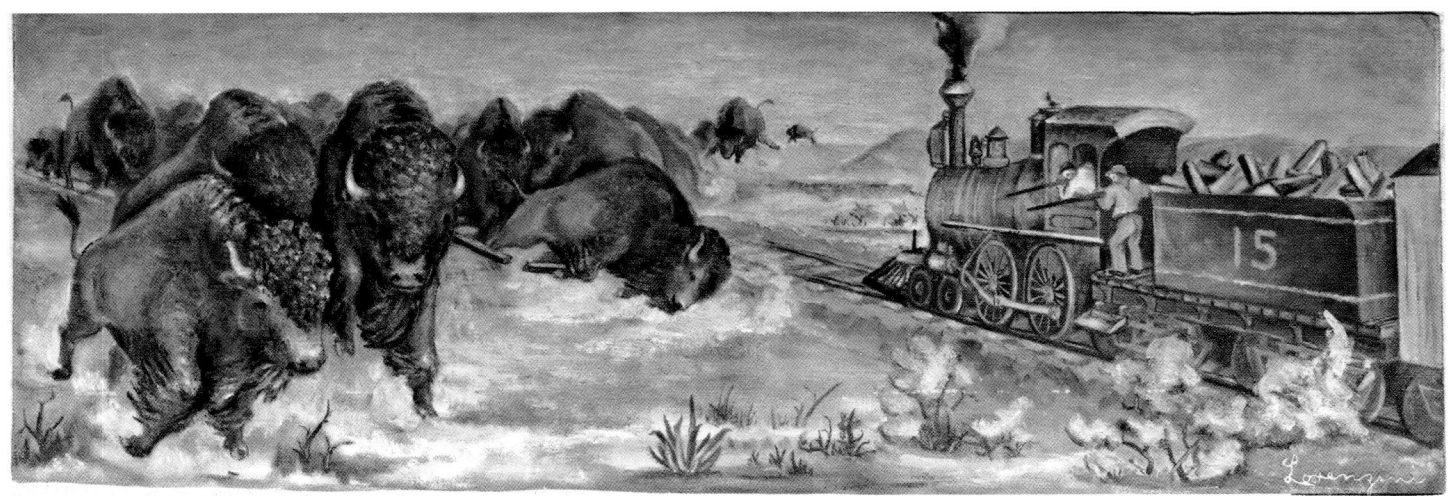

One of Lorezini's first two submittals for the
Hebron mural. From this concept she developed
a totally different composition.

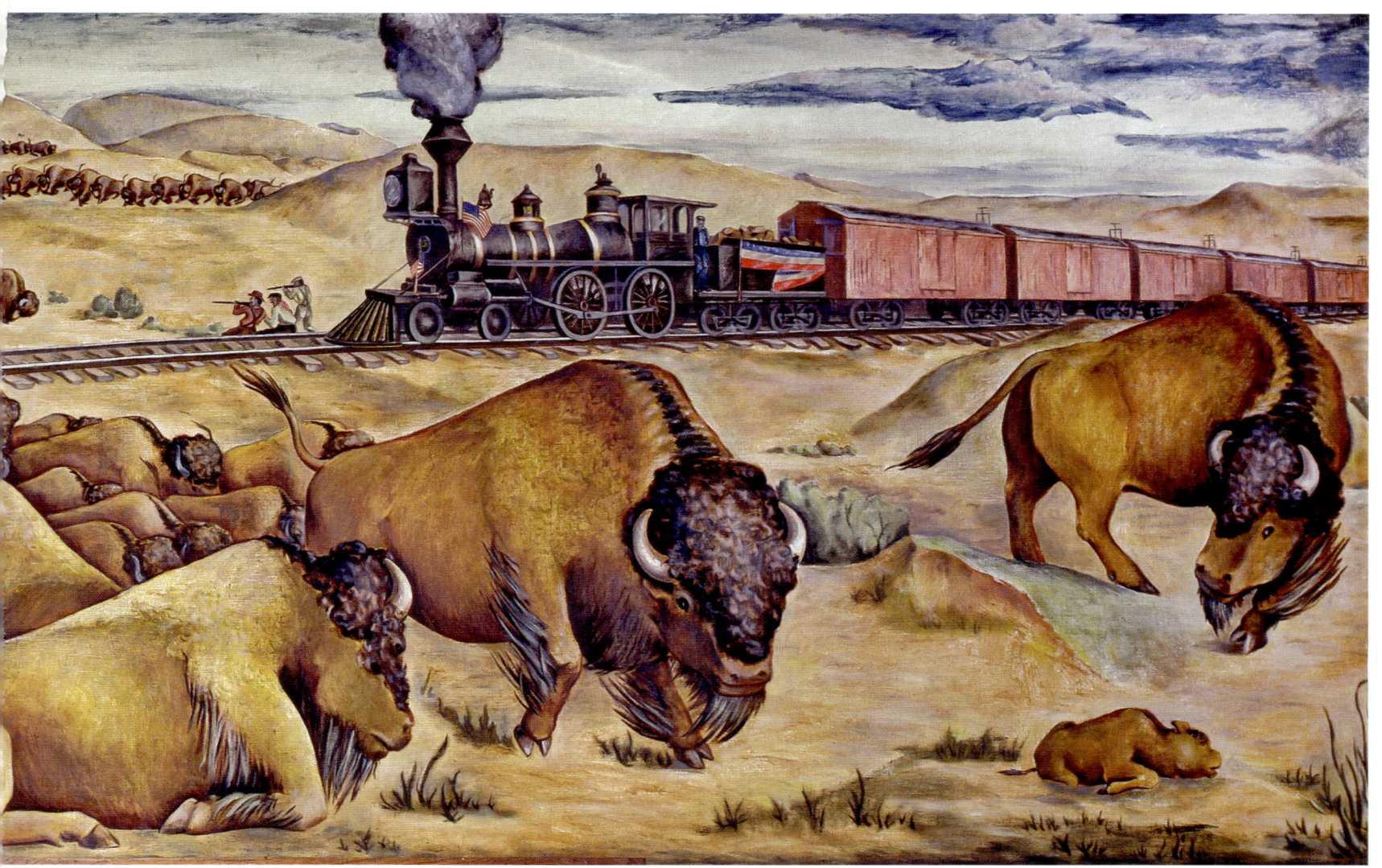

PLATE 5

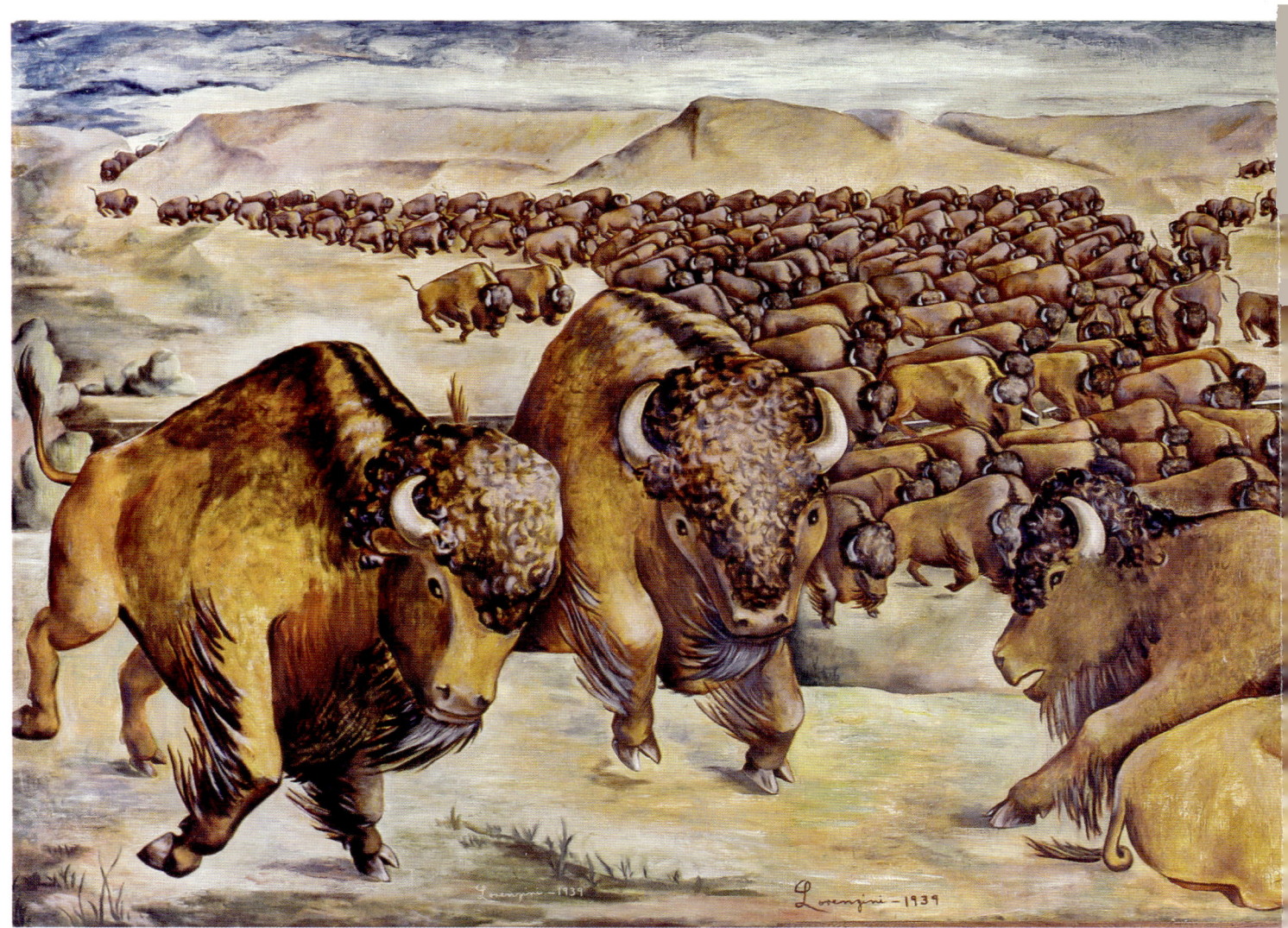

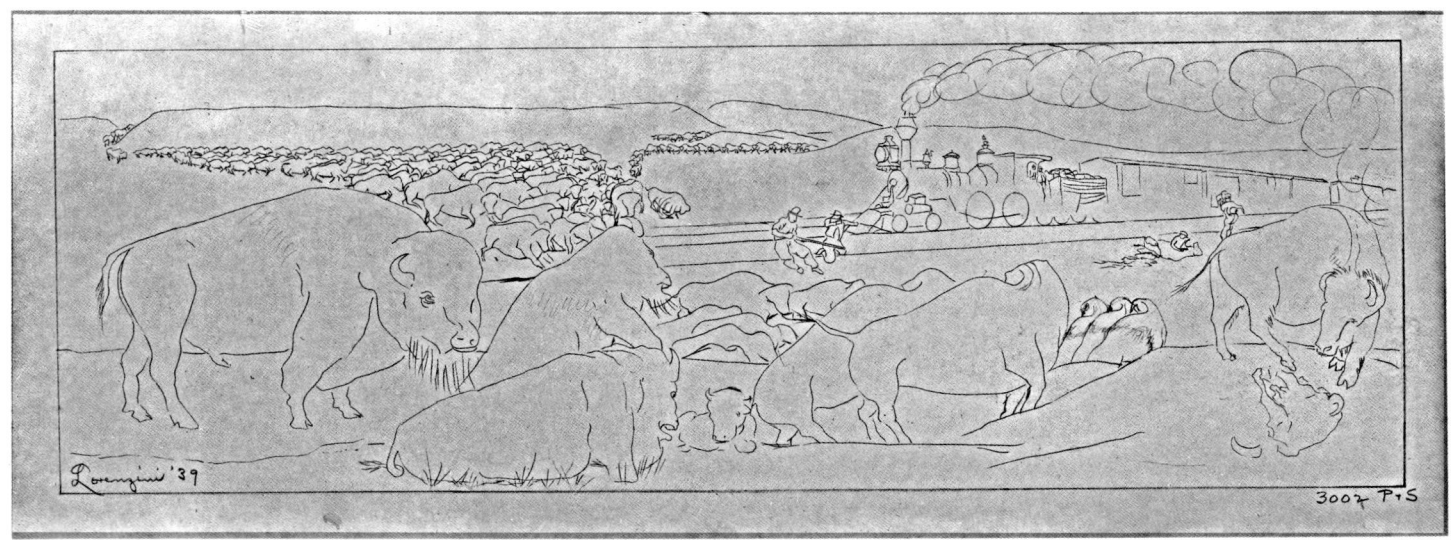

Lorenzini's sketch displeased the Section for the "anatomical lesson" of the male bison standing in the front.

Lorenzini chose stampeding buffalo based on a purported historical event. "This incident actually occurred on this spot," she wrote. "I received this information from several of the pioneers while I was in Hebron to interview the Postmaster. I also obtained this from several historical books in the college library in Colorado Springs . . . Am interested in portraying something out of the ordinary."[31] The Hebron newspaper even gave her an 1887 photograph showing a train of the period. It is unlikely, however, that this incident happened near Hebron, given that the first railroad arrived in 1884 and the great herds of buffalo had largely disappeared from the Great Plains by that time.

The Hebron mural was Lorenzini's first experience with the Section, and she entered a lengthy "correspondence course" before completing it. More than a year passed from her selection until installation of the completed mural—even though the mural itself took only three weeks to paint. She began with the submittal of two sketches. Of the two designs, the Section preferred the one showing animals on a larger scale. "[W]e wish to congratulate you on the interesting choice of subject matter," Rowan wrote. "The only suggestion offered is that further study is needed in the building up of the animals' immediate center from the enframement on up in order to make their attitudes convincing."[32] Thus began a long series of pointed and sometimes severe criticisms.

When Lorenzini submitted her preliminary sketch, Forbes Watson asked that the "anatomical lesson" of the male bison be eliminated. Rowan concurred that showing such details "is not considered in good taste for the decoration of a Post Office." He was also displeased by the image of a skinned buffalo. "The gory detail of this adds but little interest to the composition and is not acceptable." He asked Lorenzini to submit another color sketch with more study given to the animals. To comply, she visited the Cheyenne Mountain Zoo to observe buffalo firsthand. Though the animals were shedding at the time of her visit, she was optimistic that "by the time I'm ready for the cartoon they should be over this stage."[33]

Rowan was not pleased with the new color sketch: "I am somewhat amazed, however, at the lack of quality in the actual painting . . . I wish to be perfectly frank in the matter in stating that photographs of your previous work indicated more ability than the color sketches you have submitted . . . and since it was on the basis of this work that you were invited to decorate this building I expect you to meet that quality." Rowan suggested that Lorenzini confer with Frank Mechau and other faculty at the Colorado Springs Fine Arts Center. Tempering his dissatisfaction, however, he offered encouragement: "My attitude as you must know is not to discourage you but to try to help you if I can and assist you in getting your work approved." Lorenzini took her work to Boardman Robinson, director of the center, and expressed her own frustration in a reply to Rowan: "As a matter of fact, he [Robinson] was very much interested in my line drawing . . . The only reason I revised my sketch to such an extent (against my will) is that you informed me that the buffaloes in the foreground were not convincing."[34]

Rowan replied that it was "the drawing of the buffaloes that did not seem convincing to the members of this office as well as the insistence in that early sketch on the sex of the animals which seemed to us to have been over-emphasized."[35] He further suggested that she confer with Henry Varnum Poor, who was then teaching at the center.

Although the next color sketch was a "worthy improvement," Rowan criticized the background.[36] Nevertheless he allowed Lorenzini to proceed with the full-size cartoon,

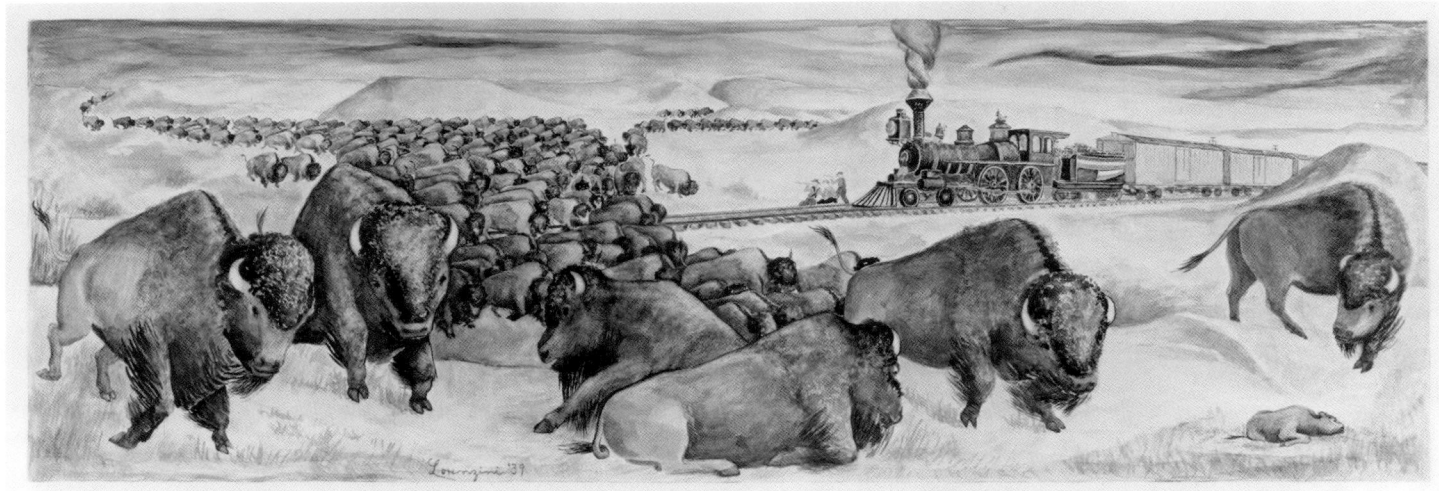

One of the color sketches submitted by Lorenzini. From a 1936 photograph.

and — nearly a year into her work — the Section released the first installment of her $670 contract.

Lorenzini followed with a photograph of the full-size cartoon, to which Rowan responded with qualified praise: "The cartoon reflects the care and study with which you have proceeded with the work." But again he suggested she check both the bison and the scale of the animals in the middle of the herd, and added that "the train track between the herd of animals and the front of the engine does not seem to lie properly on the ground."[37] Again he referred her to "experienced" artists at the Colorado Springs Fine Arts Center.

At last the completed mural was installed and Lorenzini wrote to Rowan with some apology: "Hope to have the pleasure of doing you a better job the next time as I thoroly [sic] enjoyed this commission."[38] She said the mural was well received by the community, and met with enthusiasm by the schoolchildren.

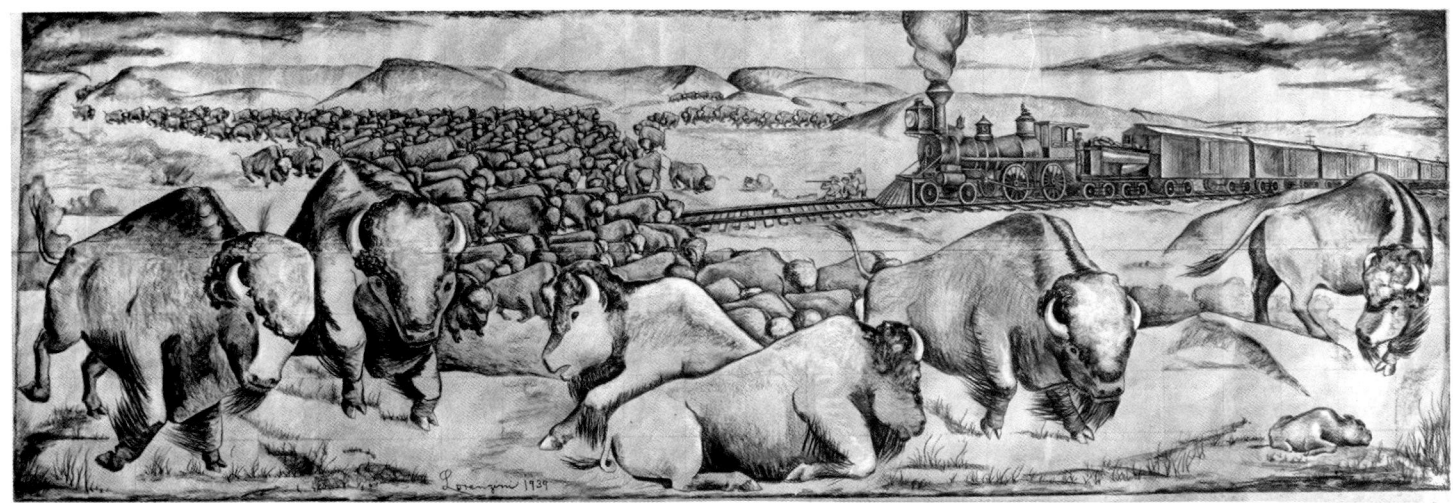

Rowan criticized the train track in Lorenzini's full-size cartoon.

BORN IN COLORADO, Eldora Lorenzini studied at Colorado State Teachers College in Greeley, and earned a master's degree in fine arts at Yale University. She also worked for the WPA Federal Art Project's Index of American Design, which was established to document America's decorative and folk arts with detailed paintings. While studying at the Colorado Springs Fine Arts Center she worked with Frank Mechau and his other students on the Colorado Springs post office mural (a project of the Treasury Relief Art Project), and Mechau's mural for the Washington, D.C., post office department building. She studied with Boardman Robinson, George Biddle, Peppino Mangravite, and Henry Varnum Poor at the center. She went on to be an illustrator, designer, and teacher. The Hebron mural was her only commission from the Section.

William E. L. Bunn (1910–2009)
Military Post on the Overland Trail

1938, OIL ON CANVAS

The most meticulous and, arguably, most historically accurate of the Nebraska post office murals is William E. L. Bunn's depiction of Fort Kearny for the Minden post office. This was the first of the murals to be commissioned in the state. Presented as a bird's eye view in blue-greens, the subject represents itself under a broad horizon. A procession of conveyances along the bottom of the mural has been likened to beads on an abacus.[39] The fort was named in honor of Stephen Watts Kearny, a prominent army officer, but Bunn, like many others, misspelled the fort's name as "Kearney" in his inscription at the bottom of the mural. The painting itself, however, is an accurate composite of buildings variously constructed during the fort's active service, based on much study and done with precision by the artist.

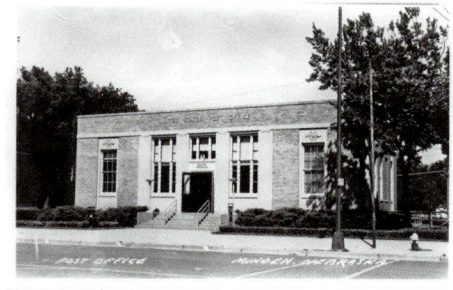

The Section invited Bunn to paint a mural for the Minden post office on the basis of previously submitted work. To the Section's approval, Bunn announced that he planned to visit the community to collect "historical and civic background."[40] While in Minden he learned old Fort Kearny had been an important outpost on the Oregon, California, and Mormon trails, and spent three months studying the subject. The "Fort Kearney Memorial Association" had acquired a portion of the site in 1928 and turned it over to

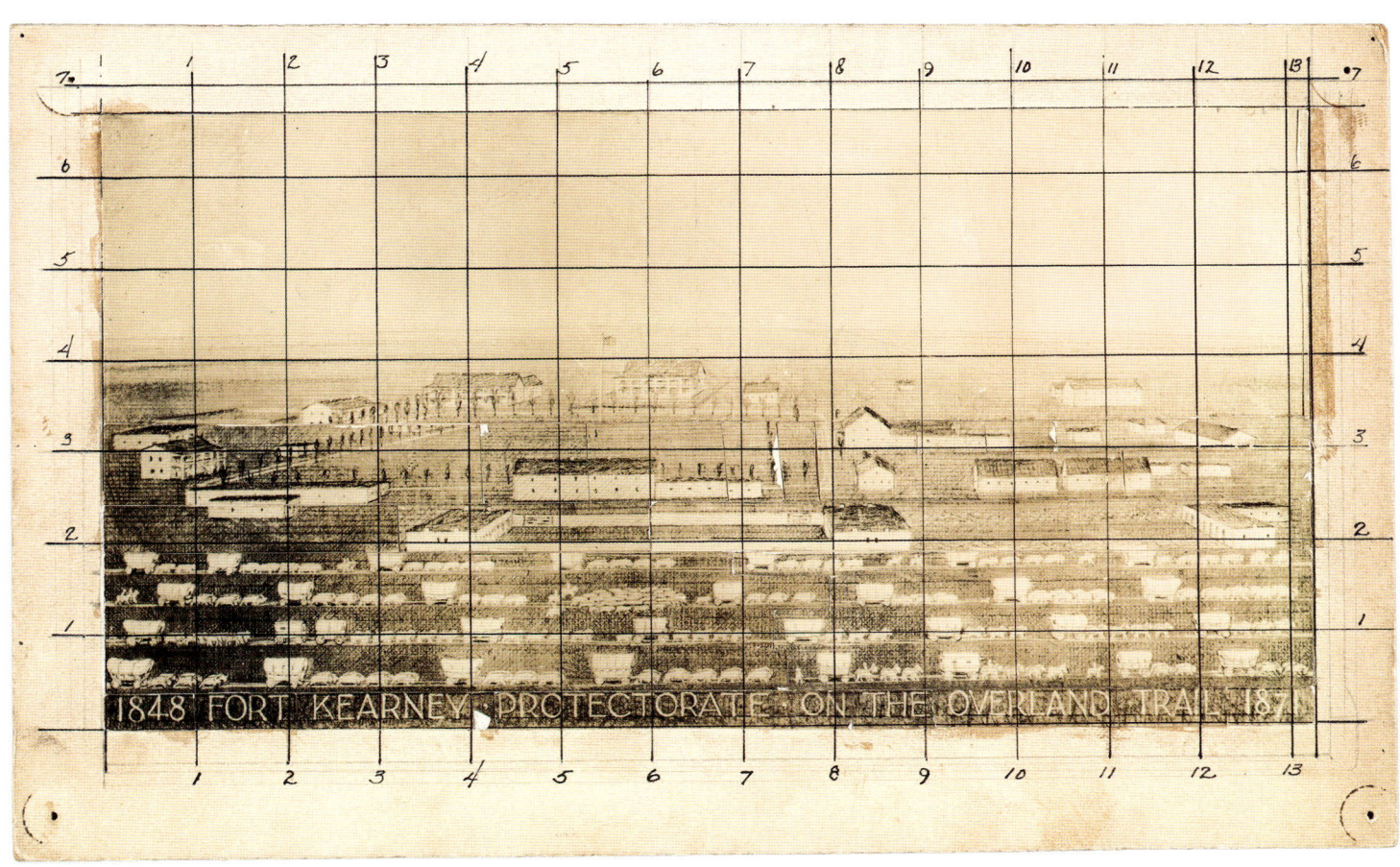

Bunn's study in two-inch scale for the Minden
mural. Rowan suggested that the horizon be lifted.

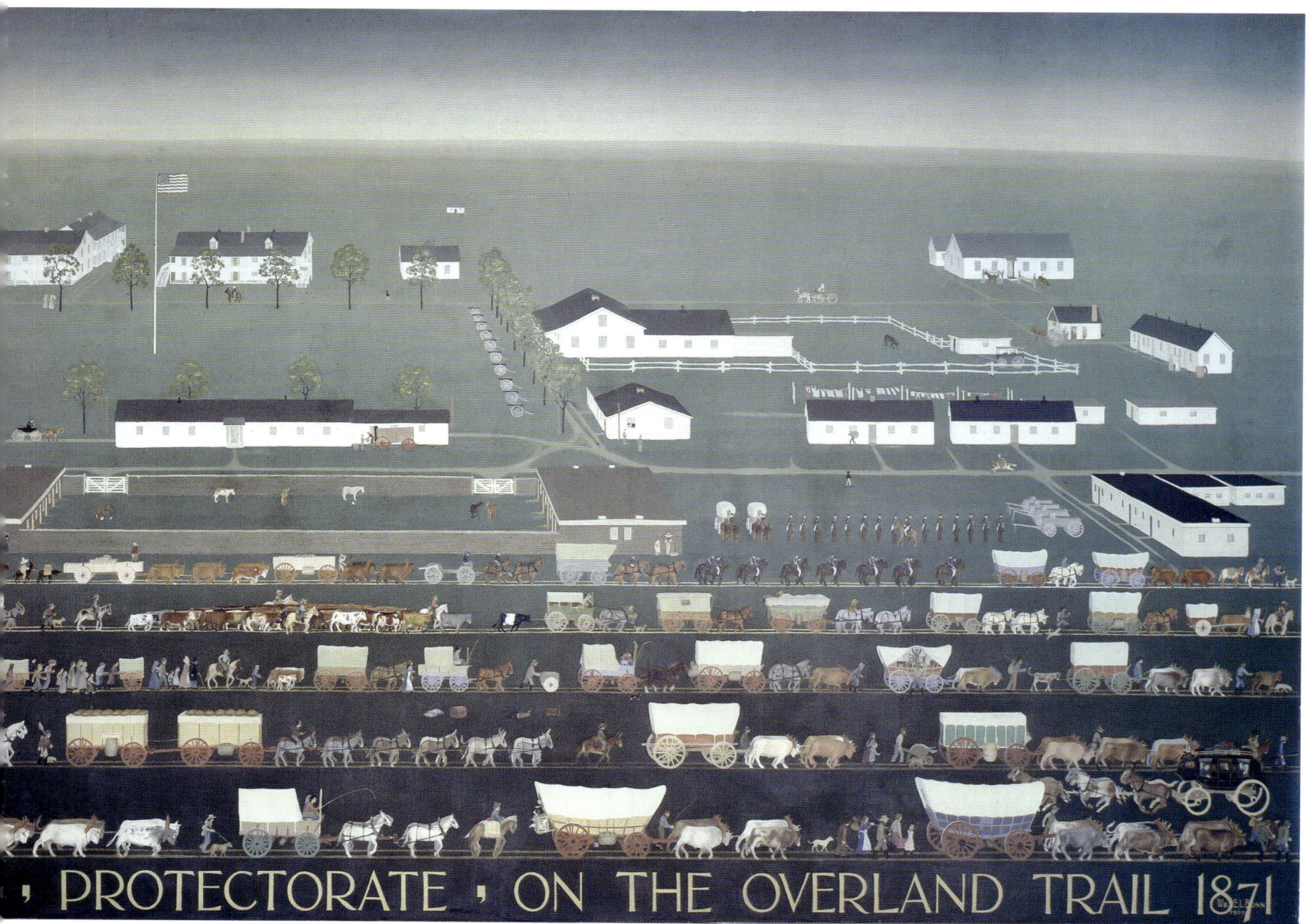

PROTECTORATE · ON THE OVERLAND TRAIL 1871

PLATE 6

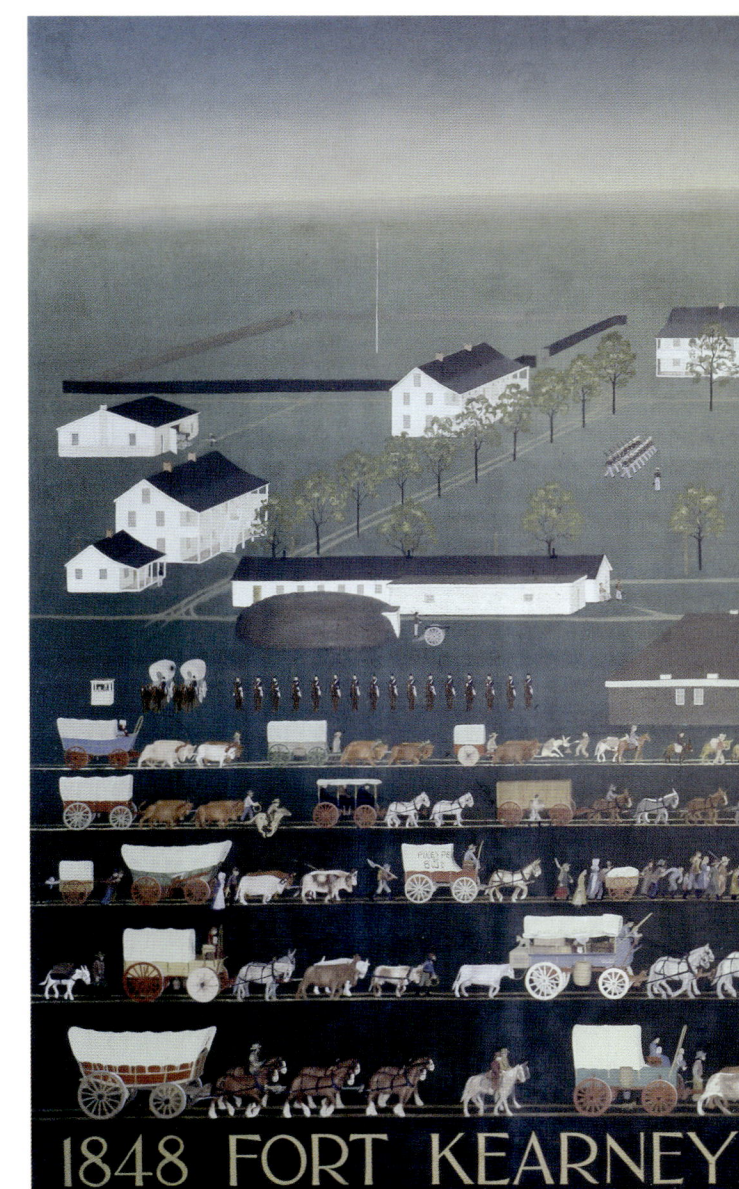

1848 FORT KEARNEY

the state of Nebraska the following year. At the time, the fort consisted only of depressions where its buildings once stood, and cottonwood trees surrounding the old parade ground. Bunn wrote:

> As instructed, I have endeavored to select a subject that is vital to the community. The residents that I have come to know in Minden seemed proud of, and ambitious to develope [sic] into a fine park . . . Together with the importance occupied by this key fort (which the citizens like to mention) in the westward emigration on the Overland Trail, leads me to believe a picture telling this story is appropriate. . . Because some restoration will eventually be done on the site of Fort Kearney [sic], I am anxious that the mural be accurate and conform to whatever reconstruction will take place."[41]

Bunn's initial charcoal sketch was well received by the Section. "The sense of great space introduced in the design was well liked," Rowan wrote, though he suggested that the horizon line be lifted "so that the division of the landscape and sky is not quite so even."[42] For the next five months Bunn scoured drawings and information supplied by the U.S. War Department, the National Park Service, and the Nebraska State Historical Society.

Bunn spent months on his color sketch only to have it met with criticism from the Section. "The buildings as you have presented them here lack convincing solidity and the general color scheme suggested is in our estimation quite dull," Rowan said, and went on to criticize the clouds, the presentation of the trees, and "the general color conviction given to the whole design." After spending more months in preparation, Bunn submitted another color sketch, assuring the Section "that in the preparation of the full sized work, I naturally can get more accuracy in the smaller details and figures.

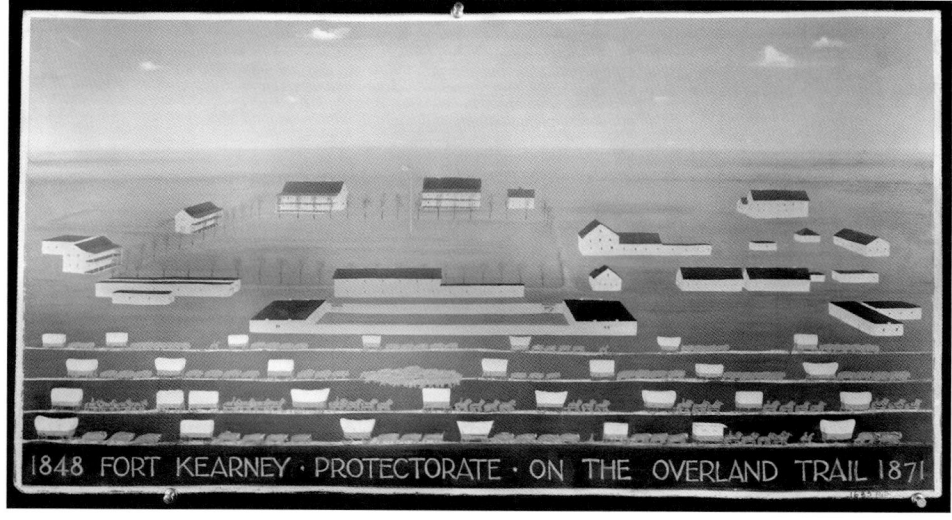

Rowan criticized Bunn's color sketch. "The buildings . . . lack convincing solidity." From a 1938 photograph.

1848 FORT KEARNEY · PROTECTORATE · ON THE OVERLAND TRAIL 1871

Possibly a stylization of grass in the darkest area of the foreground might be desirable when enlarged." He received approval to proceed with the full-size cartoon, with Rowan noting that the revised sketch was "a decided improvement" over the original. He even asked Bunn to submit the sketch to the Iowa Art Salon at the Iowa State Fair, where the Section was organizing an exhibition of artists' work for their mural projects.[43]

Bunn's sketchbook contains details of the individual buildings, wagons and teams, harness and costumes, along with notations as to the sources he used. He invited two historians to his studio to view the full-size cartoon and offer input on some of the finer details. Upon more study he asked the Section to extend the deadline: "Having seen the project move to the present stage with such care to even the smallest details makes me feel some concern that too little or too hasty work in the final stage will jeopardize quality."[44]

At last, when his completed mural was ready for delivery to the post office, Bunn wrote, "I am now content to let the mural leave my studio without any regrets for the time and efforts I put into it."[45]

The postmaster was impressed:

> We not only have gained a very decorative wall, but have revived Fort Kearney [sic] history in this community. No one knew what Fort Kearney looked like for it is over sixty years since it was disbanded. Some of the old timers feel that Mr. Bunn has been very thorough in his research and has brought back the original fort as it was in the early days.[46]

The local newspaper was even impressed by the clothes shown hanging on a laundry line, which "indicates the popularity of red underwear."[47]

After nearly eighteen months under his contract and despite the extreme lengths to which he went to ensure accuracy in the details, Bunn received only $630 — an average price awarded by the Section. When his color sketch was displayed in the Section's gallery Rowan wrote, "An architect happened to see the design . . . and was so full of praise for what you have done in the way of a decoration in relation to architecture that I hasten to pass these encouraging words on to you."[48]

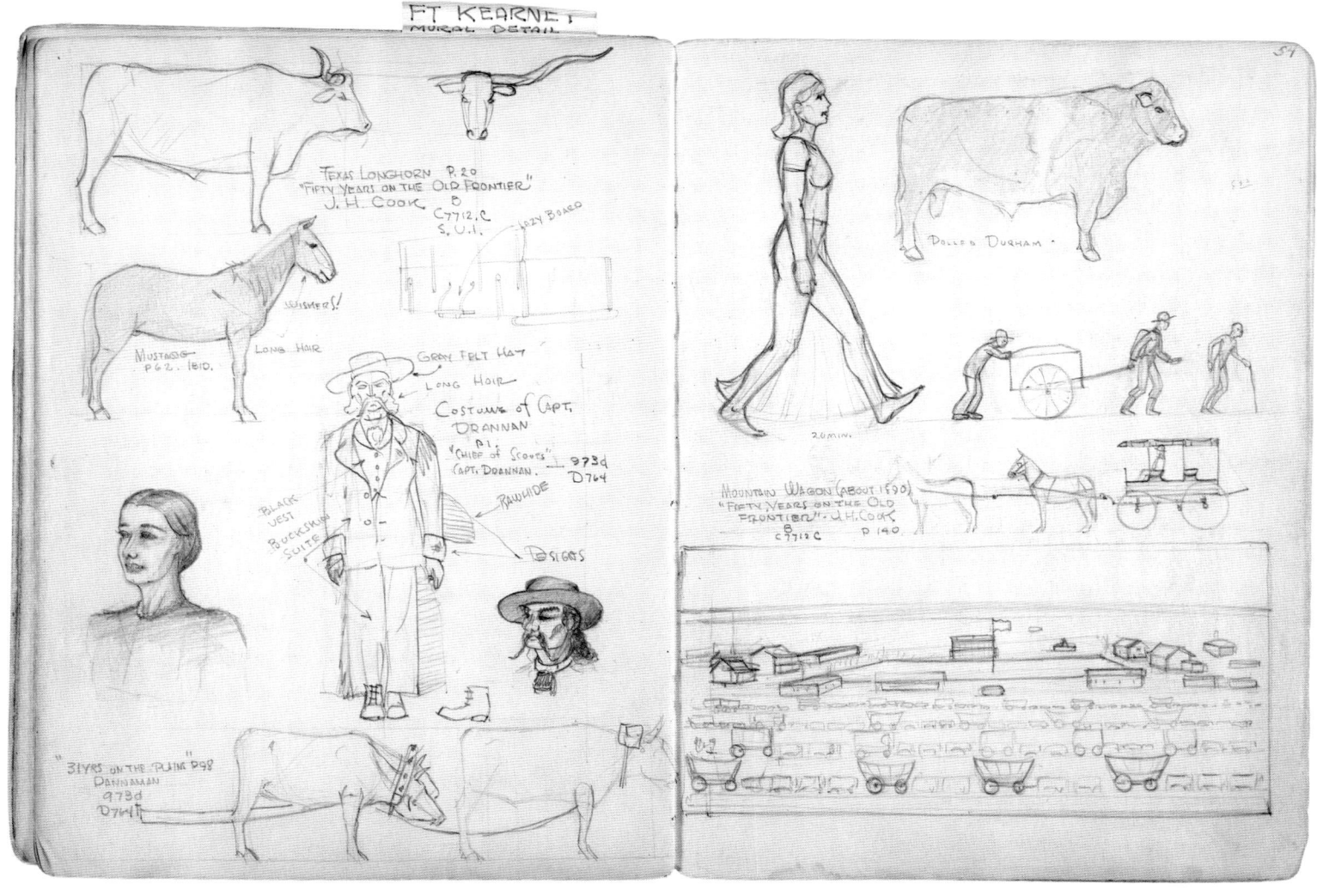

Bunn's sketchbook reveals his attempts at accuracy.

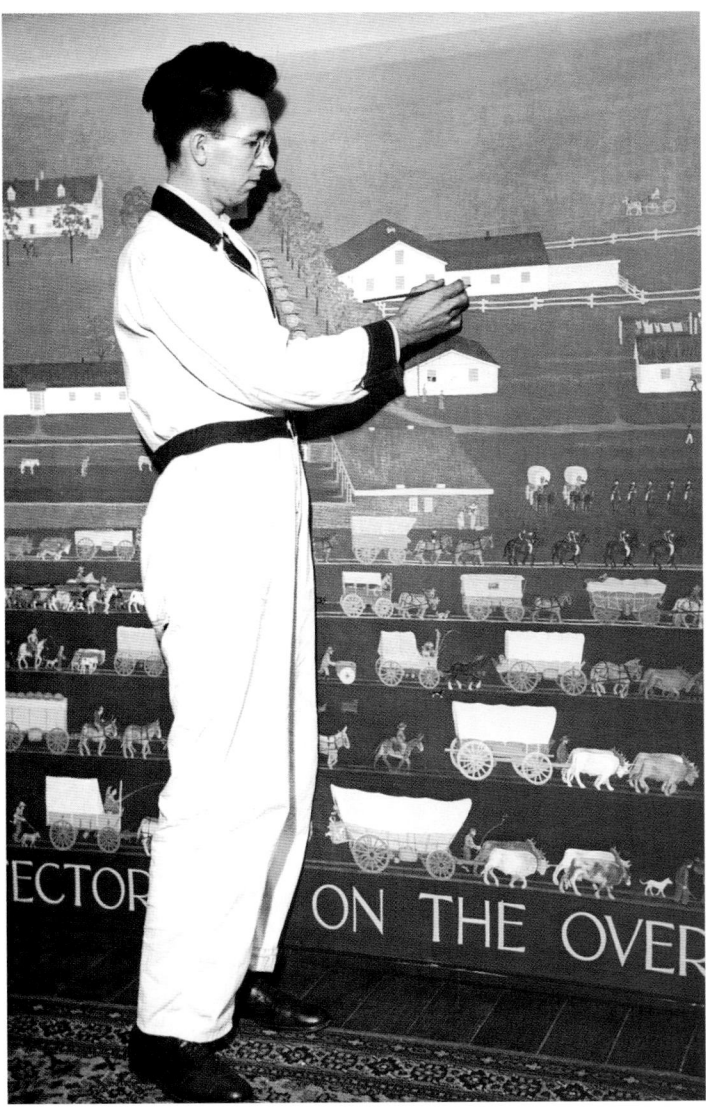

Bunn working on the Minden mural in his studio.

A NATIVE OF IOWA, Bunn was working on a Ph.D. in dramatic arts at the University of Iowa at the time of his work on the Minden mural. At the university he studied under Grant Wood. "That was the second stage of heaven," Bunn wrote of his mentor. "His style was the way I liked to work, very careful drawing, very precise."[49] His love of the Mississippi River inspired many of his works. When Wood did not enter the competition for the post office in Dubuque, Iowa, Bunn entered and was selected. It was his first important commission, and the Mississippi River scenes he created during the project were later exhibited at the Art Institute of Chicago and the Joslyn Memorial in Omaha. He went on to paint post office murals in Hamburg, Iowa, and Hickman, Kentucky, the latter being awarded under the 48 States Competition. Between 1946 and 1977 Bunn worked as an industrial designer at several companies including the Sheaffer Pen Company, where he designed pens and desk sets. After his retirement, he and his wife moved to California, where he continued to practice art.

Frank Mechau (1904–46) | *Long Horns*

1938, OIL ON CANVAS

As a youth in Colorado, Frank Mechau became fascinated with the American West. This and a mastery of compositional techniques of line, color, and space are represented in this mural, a study of longhorns being herded across the plains. The scene is dominated by the animals in the foreground that weave in and out, while the long string of cattle adds pictorial depth as it winds and fades into the distance.

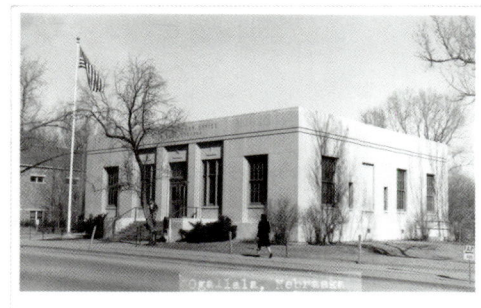

Mechau was selected for the Ogallala post office mural based on his "competent work" in previous commissions — an oft-used phrase by the Section and certainly an understatement since he was already widely recognized. His major commission, *Dangers of the Mail* and *Pony Express Riders Changing Horses* (1937) for the U.S. Post Office Department Building in Washington, D.C., was critically acclaimed. But despite his national reputation, the Section offered only an average rate for the mural, $670. He was nevertheless pleased: "I'm tickled as can be to have at the Ogallala P.O. job. I'm familiar with the country & with the history concerning it . . . just the kind I like." Rowan suggested doing something related to the new dam being built near Ogallala, but Mechau favored a cattle drive of Texas longhorns. This had been the subject of his unsuccessful entry in the Dallas post office competition, a lucrative $7,200 commission for three murals. Further inspiration

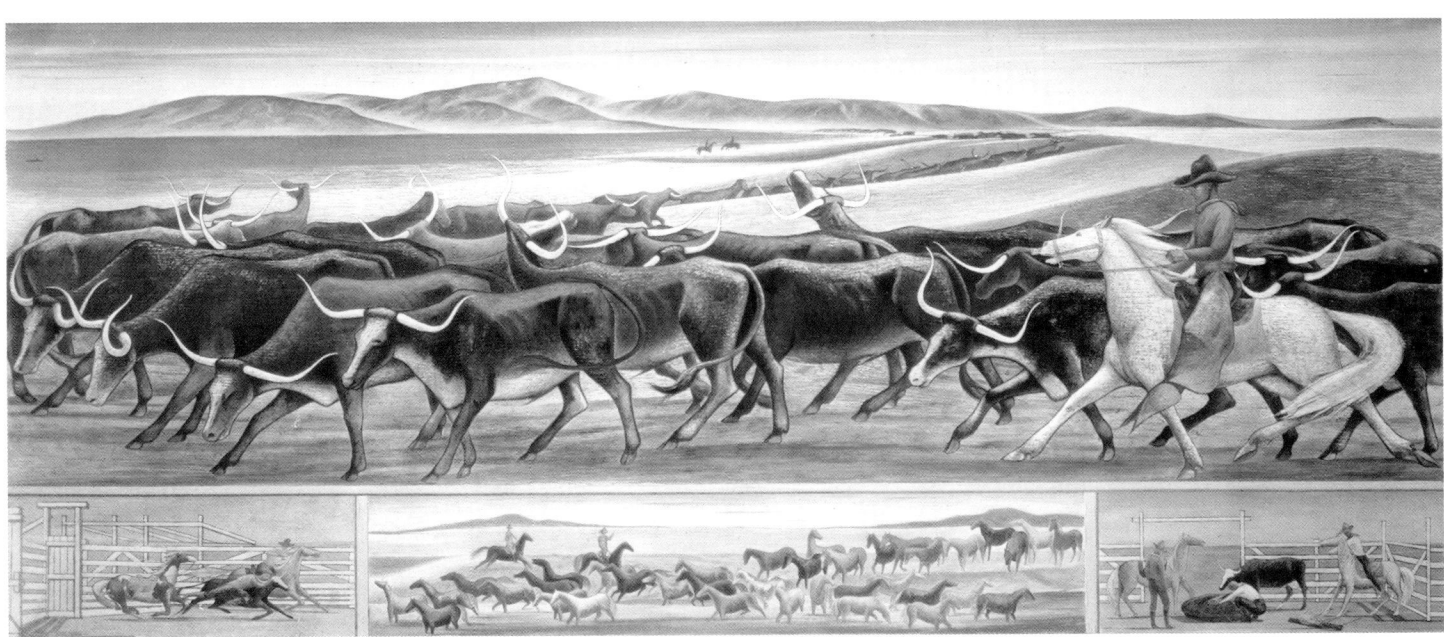

Mechau's entry for the Dallas post office competition included predella at the bottom, which the
artist deleted in his final work for the Ogallala
post office. He also reversed the tonal scheme
of the front figures and the background.

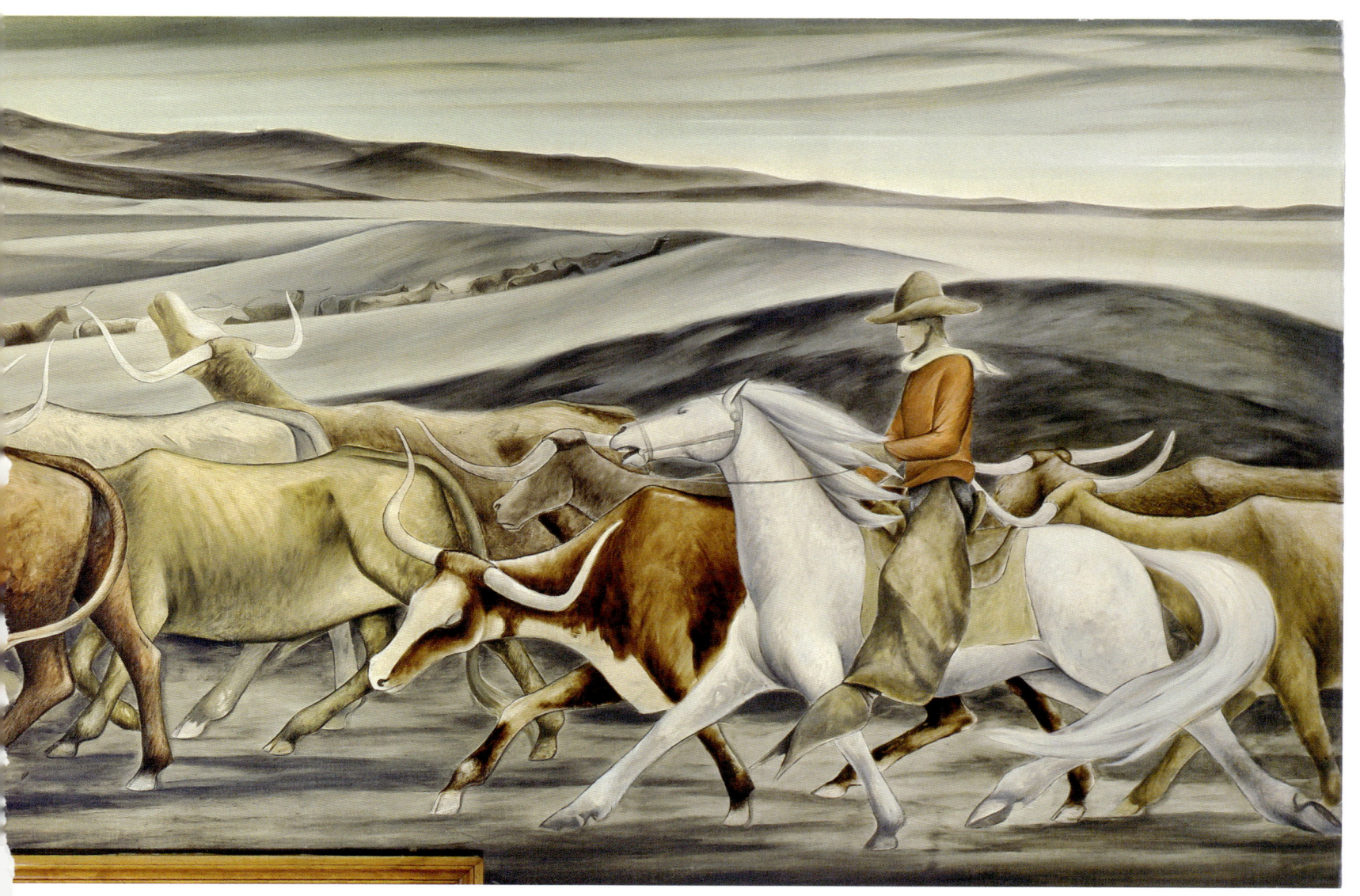

PLATE 7

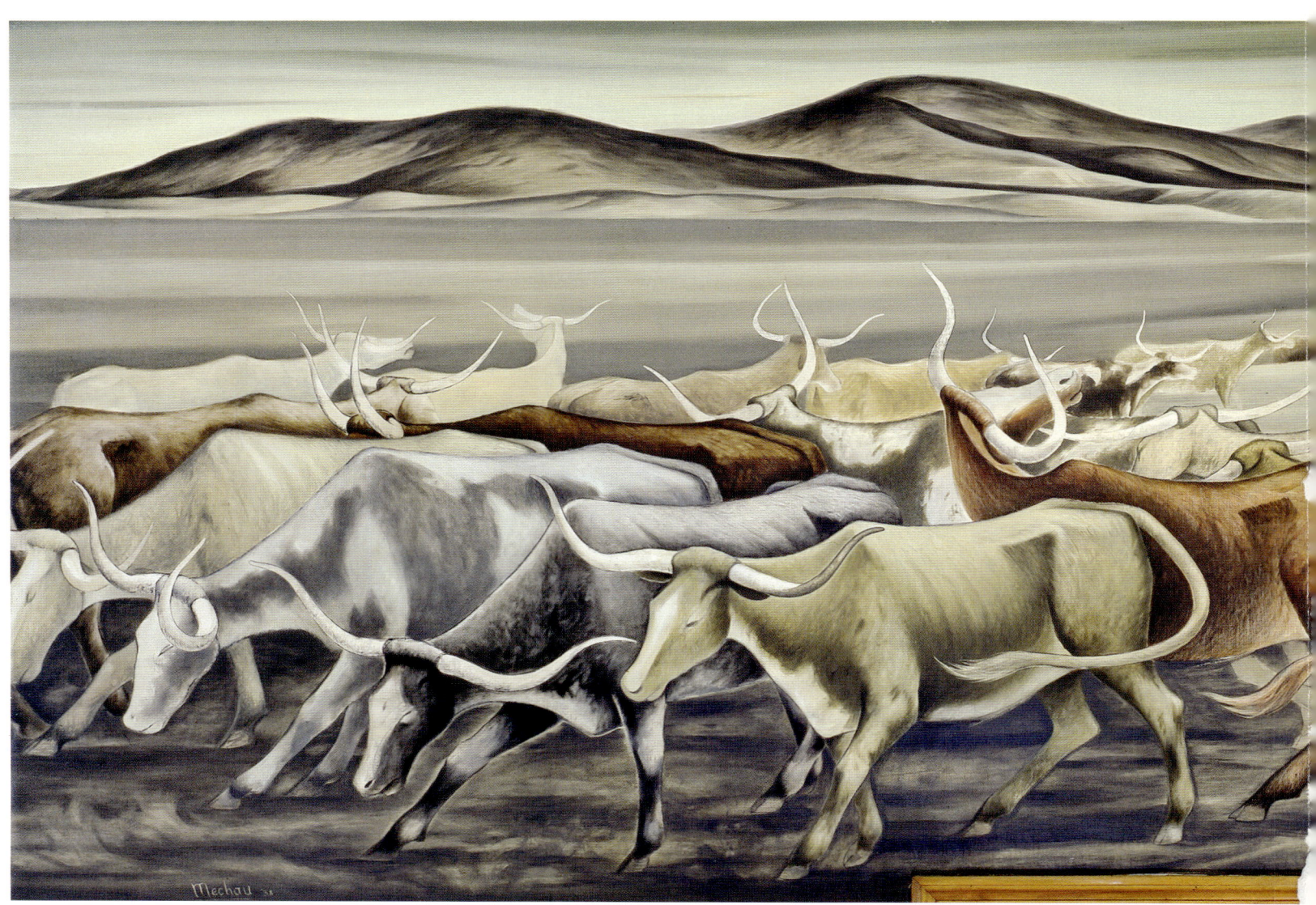

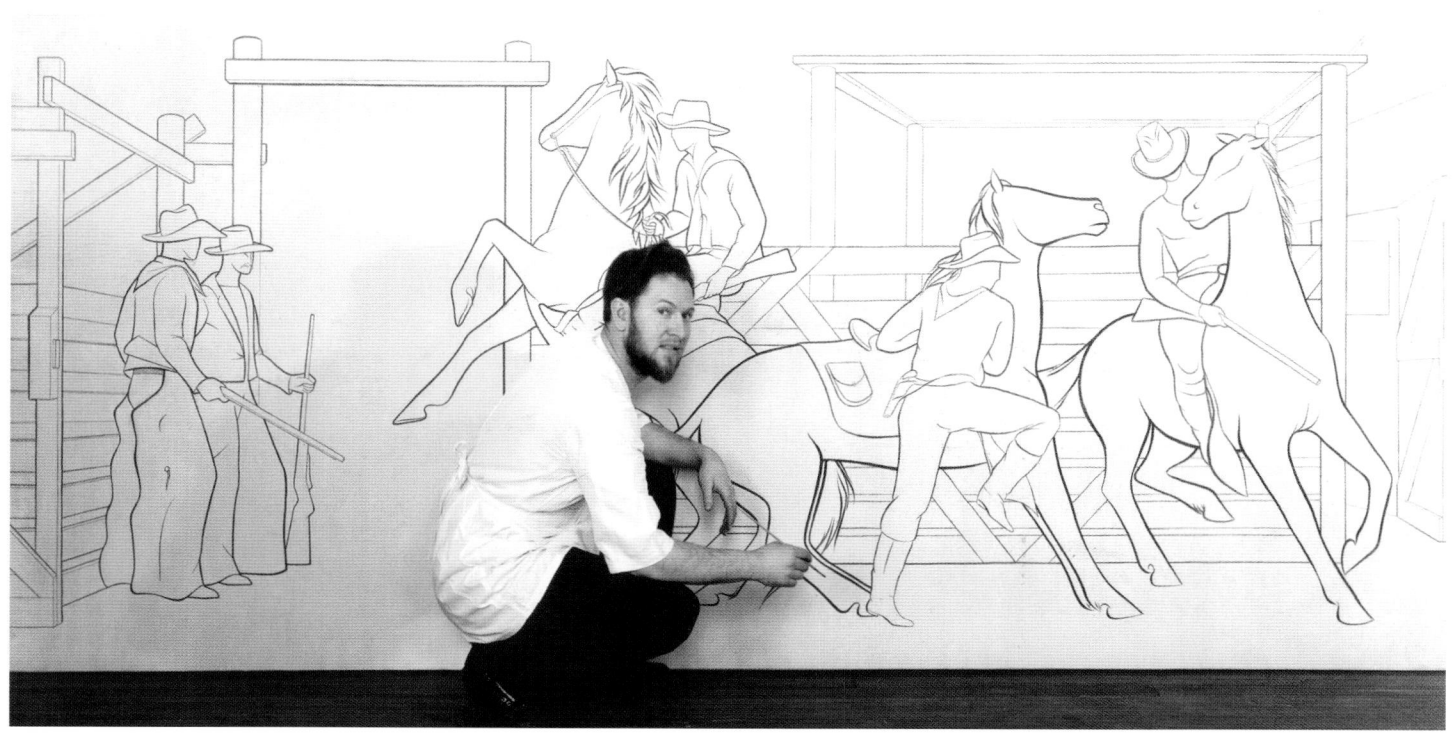

Frank Mechau works on his full-size canvas of
The Corral, one of two murals he completed
for the Colorado Springs post office under the
Treasury Relief Art Project.

came from Mari Sandoz, Nebraska author and chronicler of the West, who had written the critically acclaimed book, *Old Jules*. Mechau met Sandoz at a lecture he delivered in Lincoln and spent many hours with her, learning interesting "facts and fictions." He was impressed that Ogallala was the end of the Western Trail, "where the trek of the longhorns ended in feeding, dehorning, and shipping . . . And is this an exciting theme."[50]

He telegraphed Rowan that in the longhorn study submitted in the Dallas competition he preferred to submit the design without the predella, the small vignettes at the bottom. Mechau wrote that it made the proportion "exact."[51]

After seeing a photograph of Mechau's Dallas entry, Rowan authorized him to proceed, and offered only minor criticism of the subsequent full-size cartoon: "[T]he heavy band of animals was a little low in placement . . . and that by slightly raising this band of pattern the balance of the composition would be more satisfying." At his own preference Mechau reversed the tonal scheme in which the linear mass of animals was dark against a light backdrop, to a scheme in which the herd was light against a dark landscape. "[I]t makes the foreground forms more important & less heavy," he explained.[52]

The mural was well received by the public. When it was being installed Mechau wrote, "The Oldtimers stood about most of the day pretty much impressed with the big 'hand painter.'"[53]

FRANK MECHAU WAS BORN in 1904 in Kansas and spent his youth in western Colorado. His studies included Denver University, the Denver Art Academy, and a short term at the Art Institute of Chicago, but he disliked classroom methods. Rather, the athletic artist studied the beauty of the Western Slope, rode with local ranchers, and attended rodeos — experiences that would influence his painting. Nevertheless, Mechau went to New York City to pursue his career as an artist. He married and then went to Europe. After three years of study and painting, he wrote that he had "an extreme desire to get back to nature and life in Colorado and I should not be so remote from it." Upon his return he taught for a short term at the Kirkland School of Art in Denver in 1933 and established his own Mechau School of Modern Art. Vance Kirkland, director of the Kirkland school, wrote, "Personally, I place great hopes for this painter."[54]

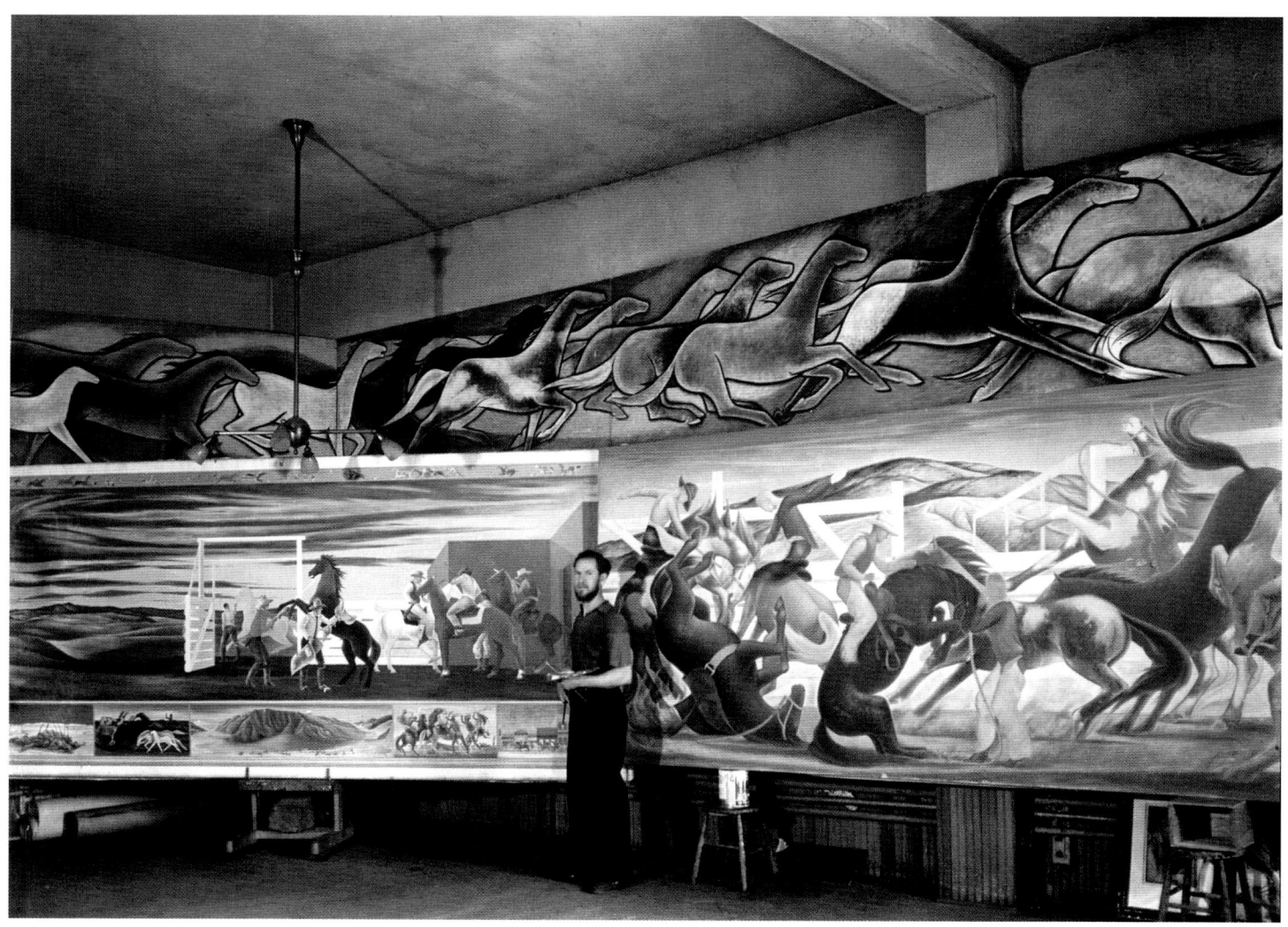

Mechau won three Guggenheim Fellowships to paint in the Rocky Mountain region. This was an amazing recognition of his talent, since the Guggenheim Foundation usually awarded fellowships for studies abroad.[55] His commission for a mural in the Denver Public Library under the Public Works of Art Project signaled his entry into mural painting. Edward Bruce lauded the artist in *Time* magazine: "Frank Mechau's paintings alone would have justified the entire PWAP program!" In another article, *Time* said of his two murals for the new U.S. Post Office Department Building in Washington, D.C.: "[T]he pride of the Treasury is in mural painting alone and in such newly-discovered talents as Frank Mechau."[56]

Under the Treasury Relief Art Project he completed murals for the Glenwood Springs, Colorado, and Colorado Springs post offices. While at the Colorado Springs Fine Arts Center he met Frank Lloyd Wright, who was apparently impressed with Mechau's ability to integrate art and architecture. Wright invited him to his school at Taliesin in Arizona. [57]

At the time of his Ogallala project Mechau received a commission for three murals for the federal court house in Fort Worth, Texas. He also completed a Section commission for the Brownfield, Texas, post office. In all, Mechau garnered six mural commissions from the Section's various projects.

From 1939 to 1943 Mechau served as head of Columbia University's sculpture, drawing, and painting department but frequently returned to the family home and studio in Redstone, Colorado. During World War II the War Department commissioned him to depict U.S. Army activities in the Caribbean and the Eastern Pacific. When the project was curtailed for lack of funds, he served as an artist-correspondent for *Life* magazine. Mechau died suddenly of a heart attack in 1946 at the age of forty-two.

Frank Mechau in his Redstone, Colorado, studio. The mural at the ceiling was a study for the fresco he painted for the garden court of the new Colorado Springs Fine Arts Center. To the left is the mural, *Pony Express Riders Changing Horses*, one of two murals commissioned for the Washington, D.C., Post Office Department Building. Behind Mechau is his mural, *Wild Horse Race* for the Glenwood Springs, Colorado, post office.

Eugene Trentham (1912–92)

Baling Hay in Holt County in the Early Days

1938, OIL ON CANVAS

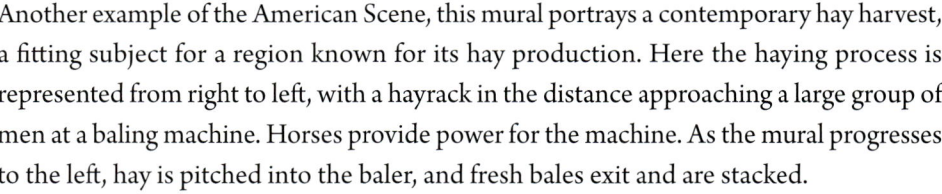

Another example of the American Scene, this mural portrays a contemporary hay harvest, a fitting subject for a region known for its hay production. Here the haying process is represented from right to left, with a hayrack in the distance approaching a large group of men at a baling machine. Horses provide power for the machine. As the mural progresses to the left, hay is pitched into the baler, and fresh bales exit and are stacked.

Trentham's use of color in this mural is unusual. He said of his works that he was always impressed by light, "an impression that has often fascinated me — namely, the vision of color one gets on a hot summer day when the sun's rays are beating down on different colored surfaces and textures." Although thought of as a cool color, he used blues to accentuate the summer heat. In approving the color sketch Rowan commented that he found the color scheme "quite unusual and certainly interesting." He authorized payment of the first installment of the $570 contract. Later, when the mural was complete, Trentham wrote that his goal had been to achieve "the tactile quality of sunlight."[58]

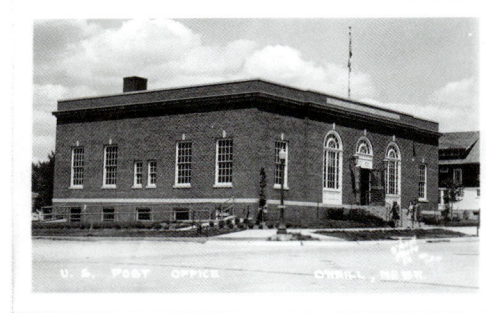

Trentham received the O'Neill commission based on his submittal for the post office in Petersburg, Virginia. His "correspondence course" with the Section included criticism for several details in the photograph of the half-finished work. "The foreparts of the

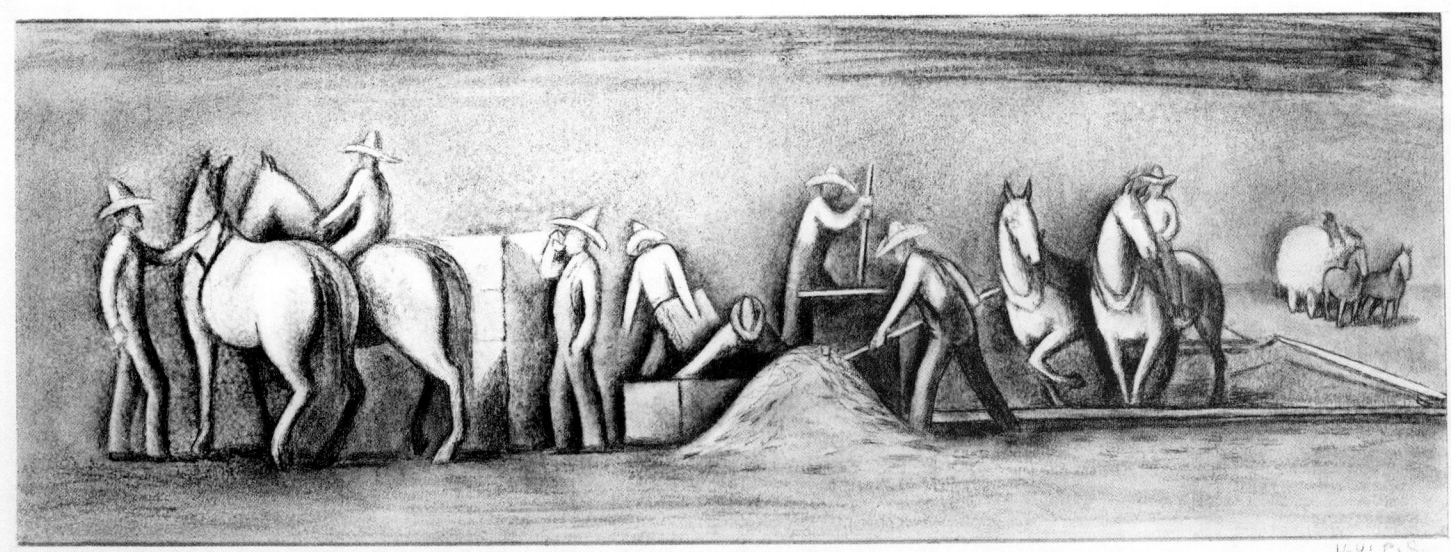

Trentham's initial study for the O'Neill post office.

second horse from the left do not seem entirely realized," Rowan wrote. "This is also true of the center figure of the man kneeling in the composition . . . the spatial relation does not seem entirely convincing."[59] Trentham agreed with the comments, but the mural had already been installed.

Rowan had one final criticism: "Unfortunately, we feel that the photograph does not represent you at your best in our records. Nevertheless, it is sufficient to inform us that the work has been installed." But the mural was well-received by the community. The postmistress wrote that it "certainly is an addition to the decoration of the building" and had received "very favorable comments." The local newspaper said it "adds a great deal to the appearance of the building."[60]

EUGENE TRENTHAM WAS A Tennessee native who moved to Denver and attended Colorado State Teachers College. He studied under Charles Kassler, who worked for the WPA and created several frescos. From 1935 to 1939 Trentham was an artist for the Mural and Easel Painting Division of the WPA's Federal Art Project (FAP). He said of the project, "I can say whatever progress I have made . . . is directly traceable to the economic security and understanding which the Project has offered me."[61] His mural for the O'Neill post office was the only work he did for the Section. He was awarded a Guggenheim Fellowship in 1939 and joined the faculty of the University of Texas Department of Fine Arts, where he taught from 1940 to 1955.

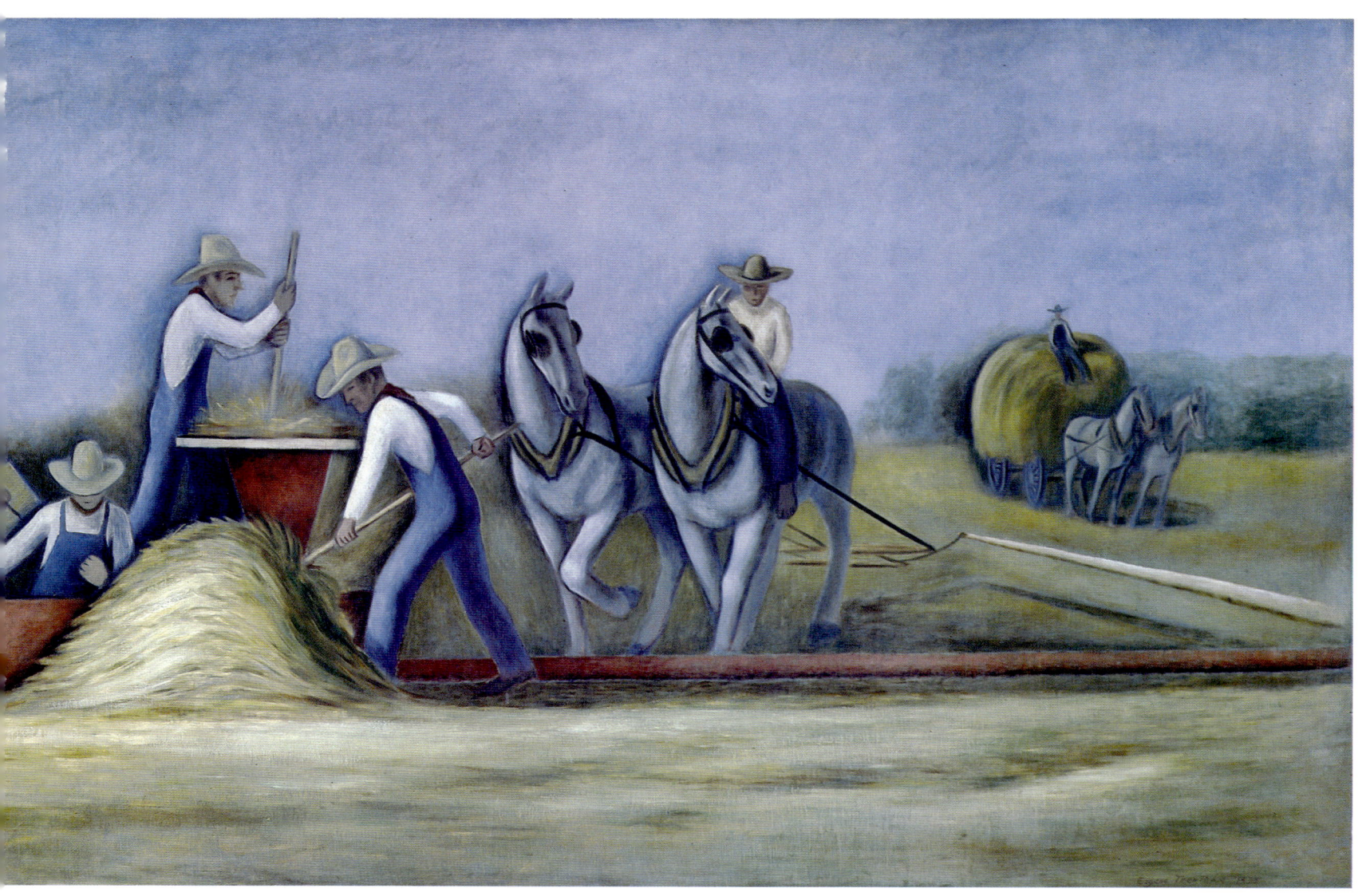

PLATE 8

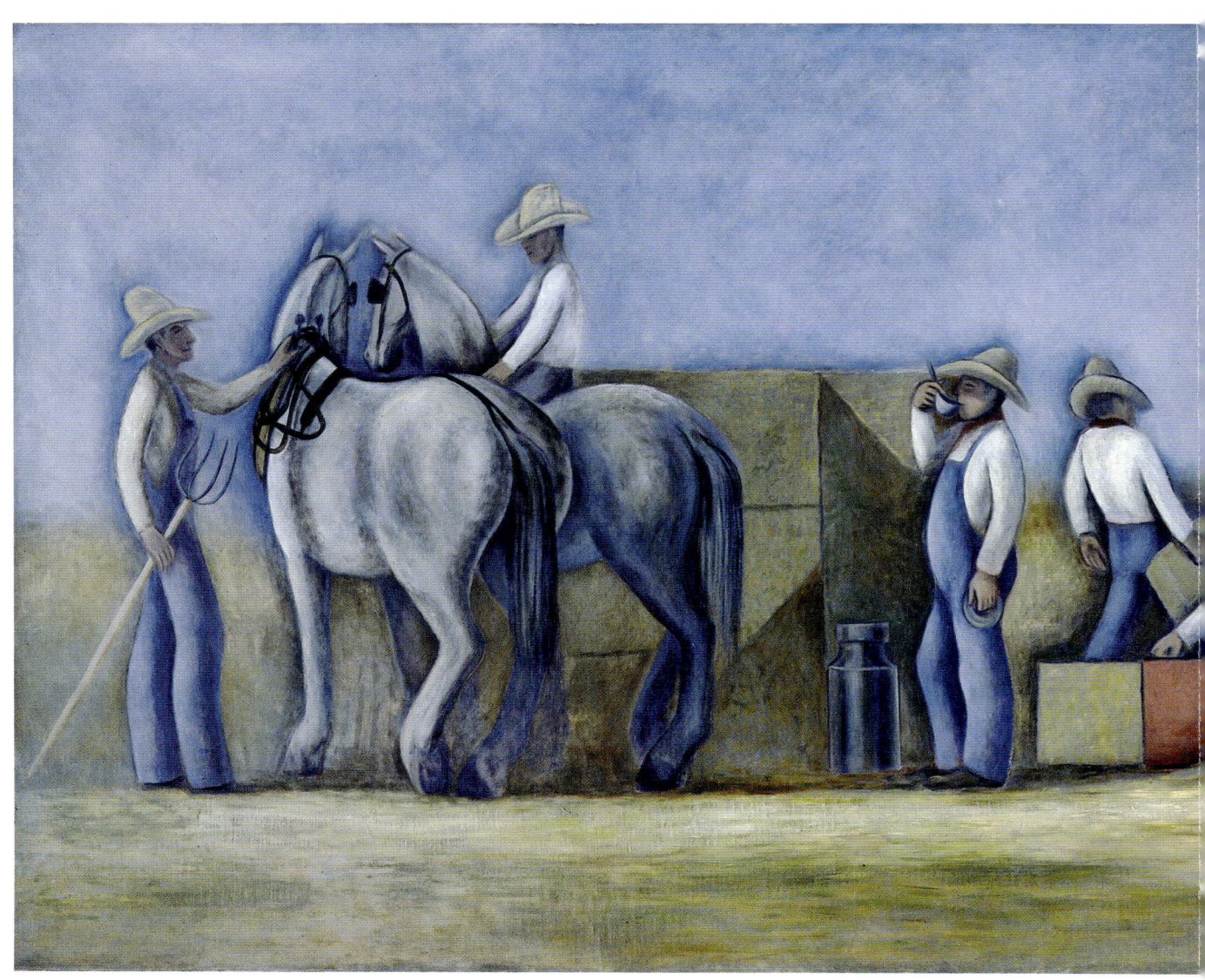

Kenneth Evett (1913–2005) | *The Auction*

1942, TEMPERA AND OIL GLAZE ON CANVAS

In his mural, Kenneth Evett captures the American Scene by portraying the social aspects of a contemporary livestock auction. Groups of people gather to exchange local news and gossip. Describing his proposed work, Evett said the community auction is "a very colorful, as well as characteristic affair in the middle west."[62]

Evett received the Pawnee City commission in 1941 based on a submittal for the South Denver post office competition. He disliked what he saw as the Section's and the public's preference for scenes of local history. Once when the postmaster in Caldwell, Kansas, insisted on a scene of cowboys driving cattle on the old Chisholm Trail, Evett lamented to the Section, "I don't like to be uncooperative but must we do historical murals indefinitely?"[63]

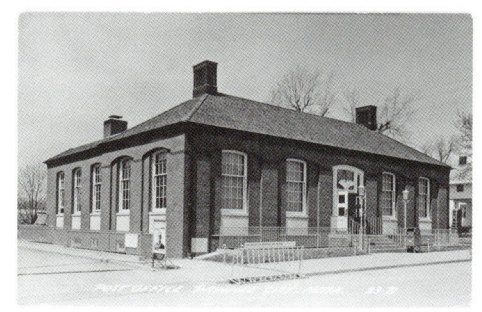

When the Section accepted Evett's black-and-white sketch, Rowan commented that it "contains great possibilities as an amusing decoration."[64] In addition to asking for a two-inch-scale color sketch, he also asked Evett to submit an architectural rendering showing how the mural would be placed in relation to other features on the wall. Both were approved under the $750 contract and Evett proceeded with the full-size cartoon and then the mural itself.

"It looks very well and the people seem to like it," Evett wrote after the installation. But despite his intent to portray a "colorful" affair, Depression realities were not far from the

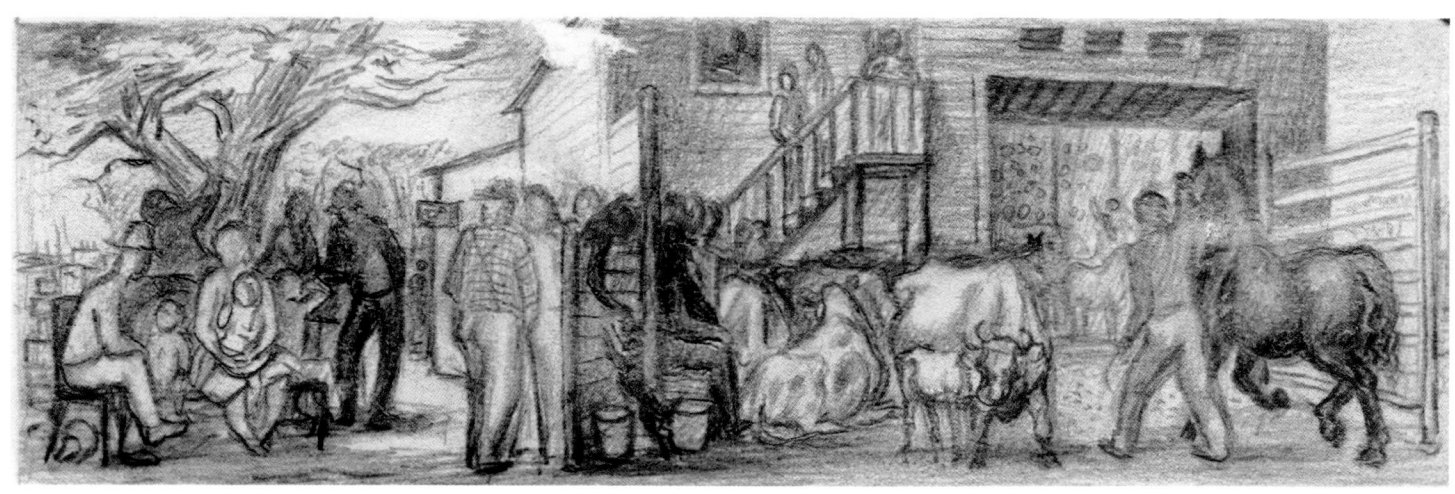

Kenneth Evett's preliminary black-and-white
sketch for the Pawnee City mural.

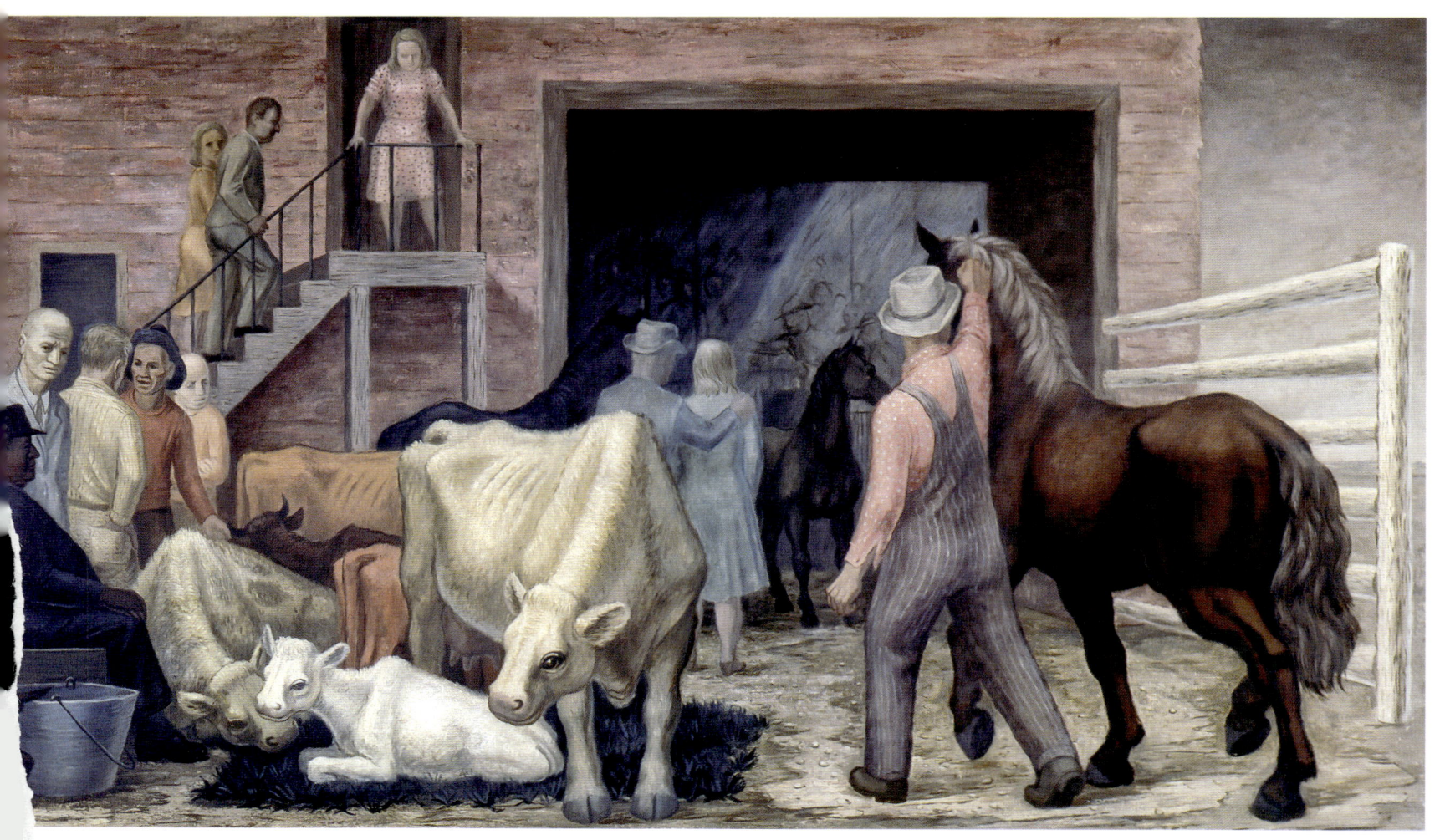

PLATE 9

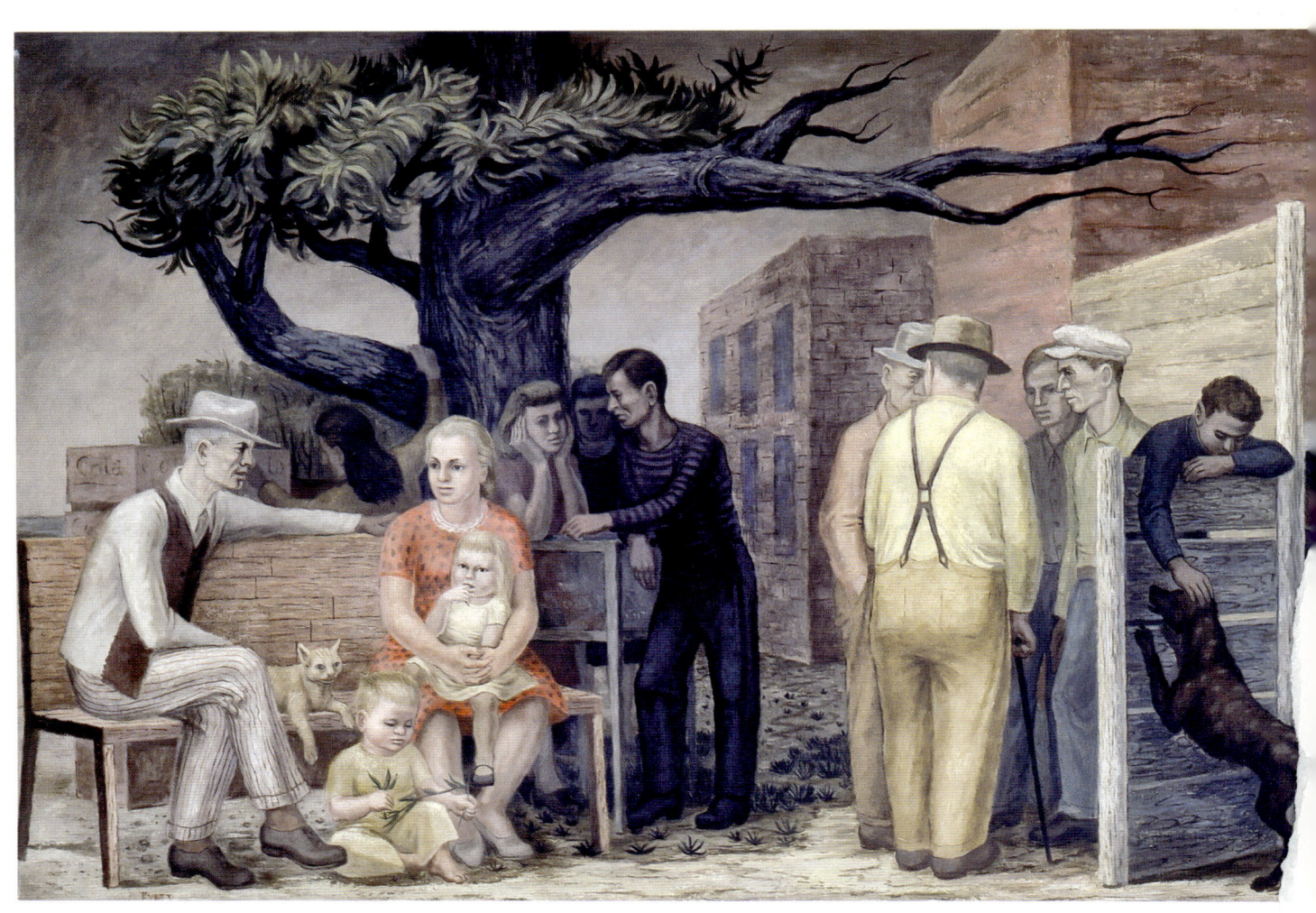

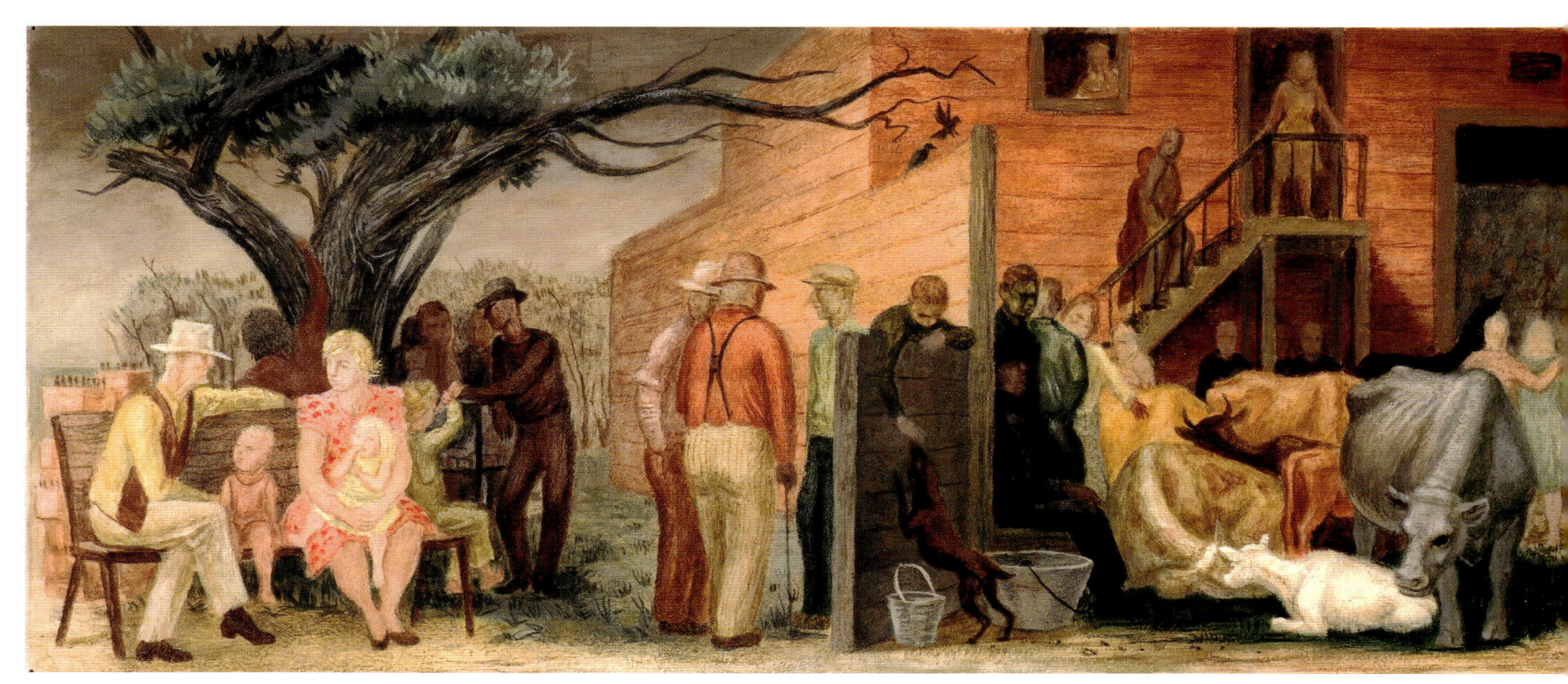

Evett's color study, done in gouache, for the
Pawnee City mural.

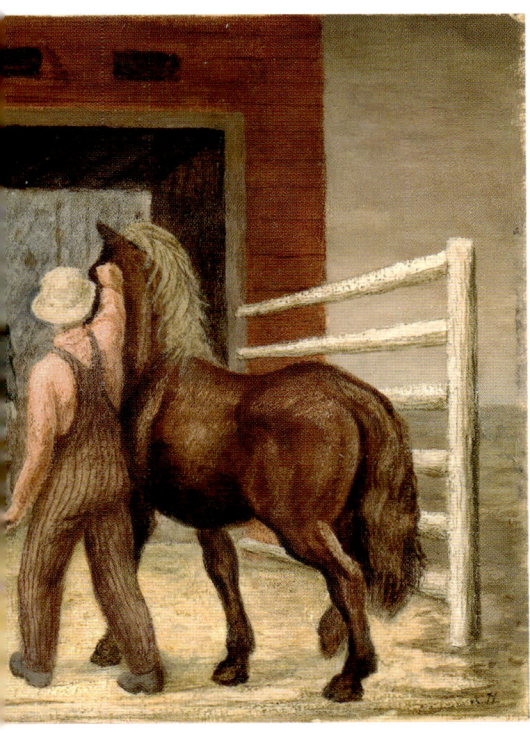

minds of the public. The local newspaper interpreted the mural differently from how the artist intended it: "[F]rom the expression on the faces it appears a foreclosure or forced sale is in progress."[65]

The Pawnee City mural turned out to be the Section's final Nebraska work. Rowan authorized Evett to proceed with a full size cartoon on December 6, 1941—just one day before the Japanese attack on Pearl Harbor.

EVETT WAS BORN IN Colorado and received a master of fine arts degree from Colorado State Teachers College. Granted a scholarship, he enrolled at the Colorado Springs Fine Arts Center in 1936. He said, "This was my first contact with the big world of art and it was very exhilarating." Evett studied under the accomplished muralist (and the center's director) Boardman Robinson and served as an assistant to Robinson, who was then commissioned for murals in the Department of Justice Building in Washington, D.C. Evett described Robinson as "one of the really big men," who also encouraged his students to enter the Section's competitions and "go out on their own." [66]

At the Colorado Springs center Evett also worked under George Biddle, Henry Varnum Poor, and Peppino Mangravite. At the time of his commission for the Pawnee City post office, he had just completed a post office mural for Golden, Colorado, and received a total of four successful post office commissions, including Caldwell, Kansas. He also produced two post office murals for Horton, Kansas. He taught at Cornell University from 1948 to 1979 and became a full professor, chair of the art department, and professor emeritus upon his retirement. In 1954 he won a national competition to paint three murals in the rotunda of the Nebraska State Capitol. He was elected to the National Academy of Design in 1994.

Archie Musick (1902–78)
Loading Cattle, Moving Westward, and *Stockade Builders*
1941, OIL ON CANVAS

Loading Cattle is dominated by a cattle car, a loading chute, and a series of corrals done in browns and red. Wranglers prod the cattle. Companion murals, *Moving Westward* and *Stockade Builders,* were commissioned for placement above the postal clerks' windows. Chief Red Cloud is mounted on a horse as he peers backwards to a fire-ravaged settler's cabin. Native buffalo are in the background and Red Cloud's people are leaving in the face of the coming settlement. Countering the scene of the disposessed Native Americans, the companion panel to the right features the construction of a frontier stockade, representing the permanence of the new settlements. And instead of buffalo, horses gallop in the background. The panels are placed in such a way that Chief Red Cloud appears to be pointing at the stockade. As in *Loading Cattle,* Musick's elongated and sinewy figures are reminiscent of Thomas Hart Benton, with whom he studied.

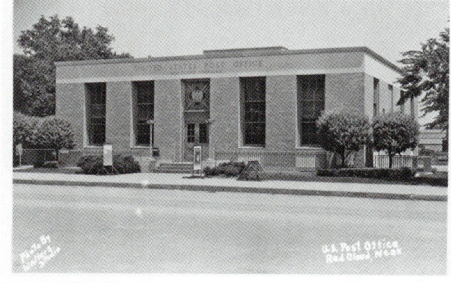

 Loading Cattle began as a study, one of two submittals Musick entered for the post office at Greybull, Wyoming, in the 48 States Competition. But a fellow student at the Colorado Springs Fine Arts Center, Manual Bromberg, nosed out Musick for the commission. However, his two studies from the competition were considered for the Red Cloud post office. For Musick, the commission fulfilled the long-standing goal of being recognized by the

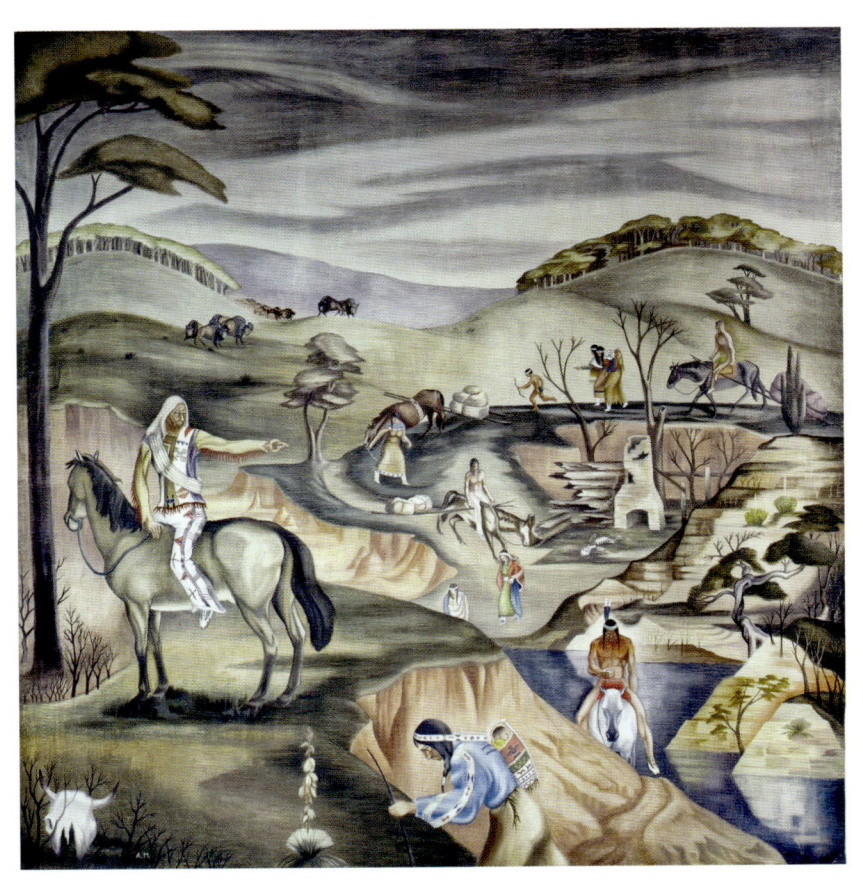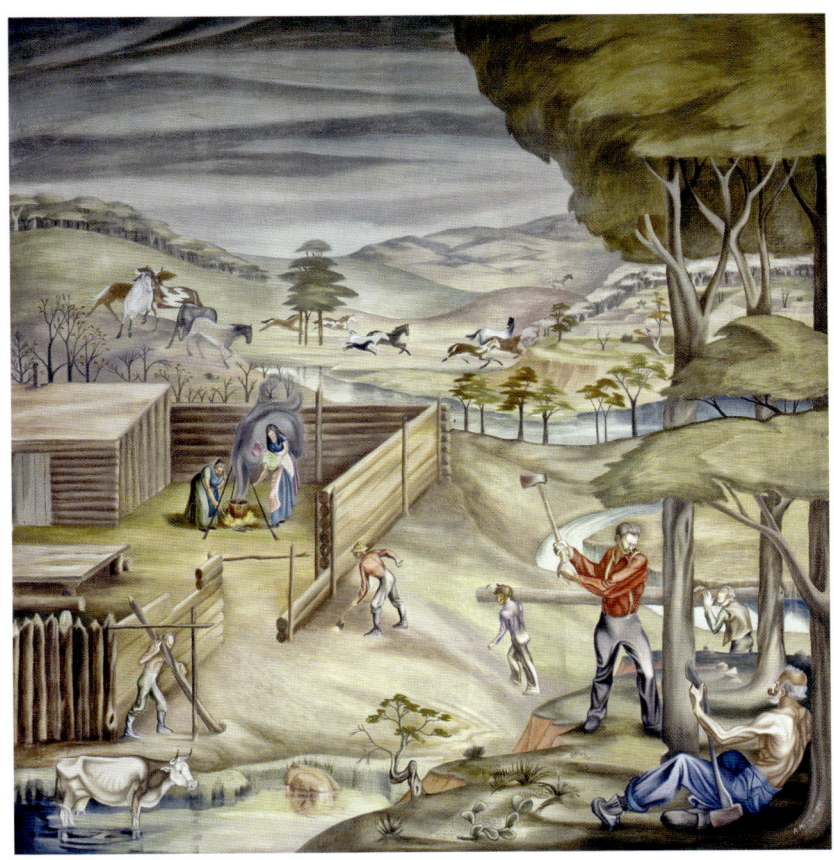

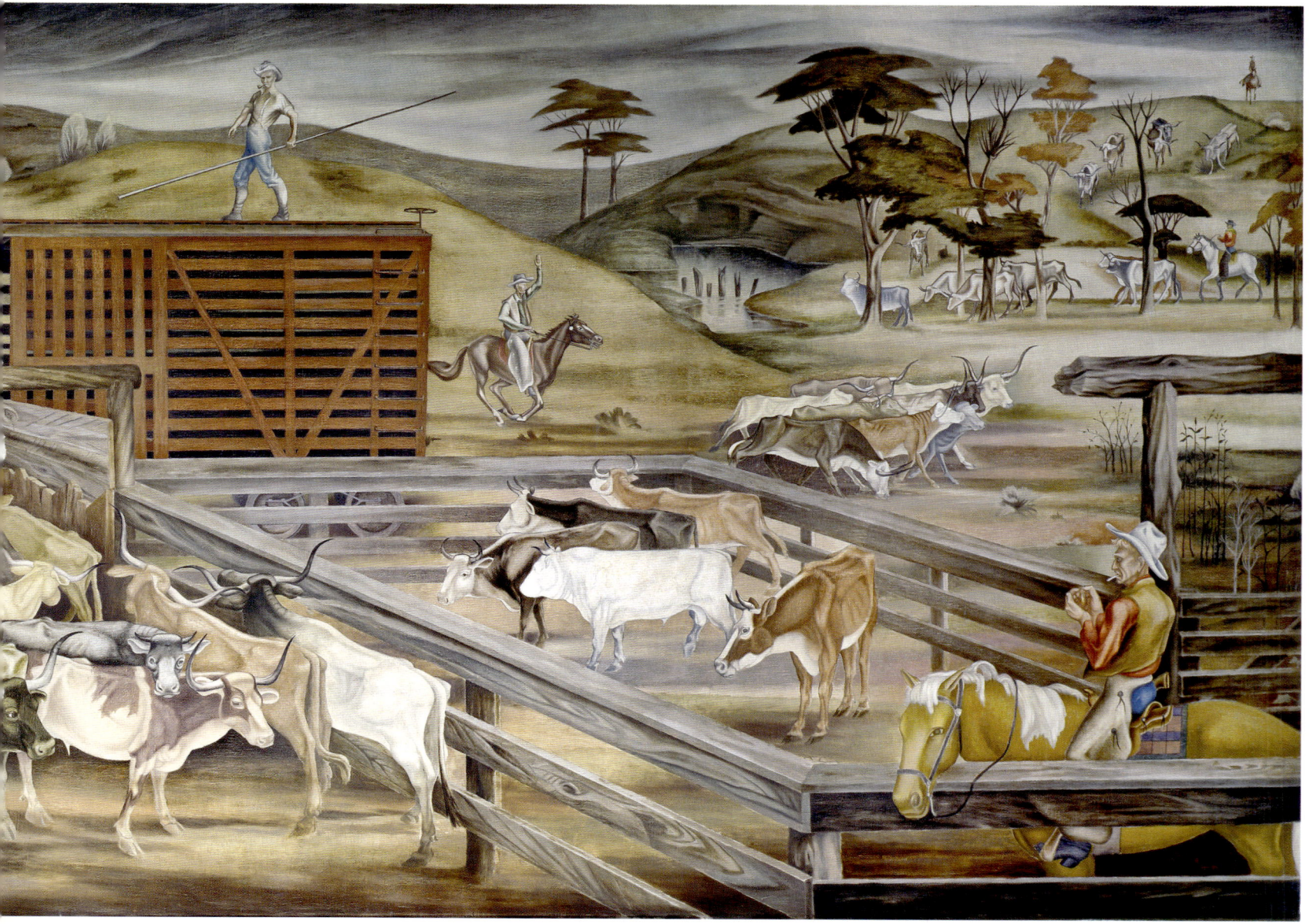

PLATE 10

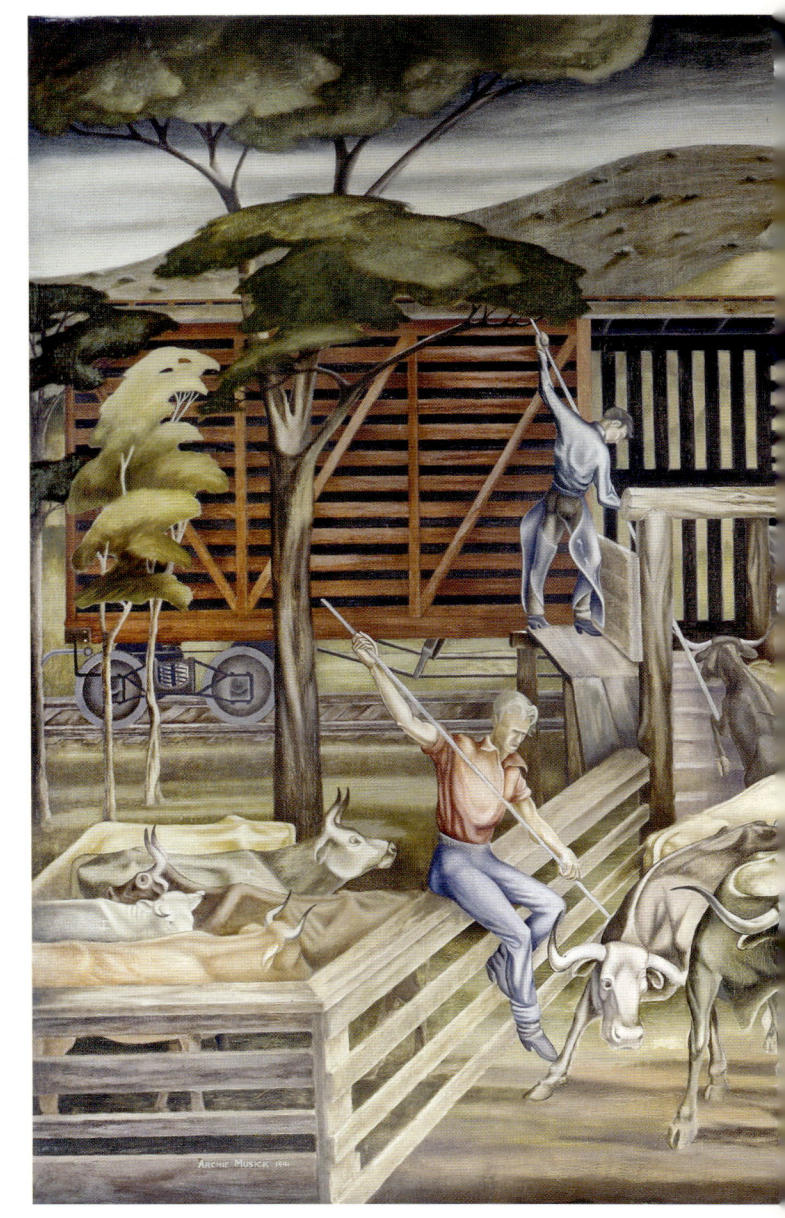

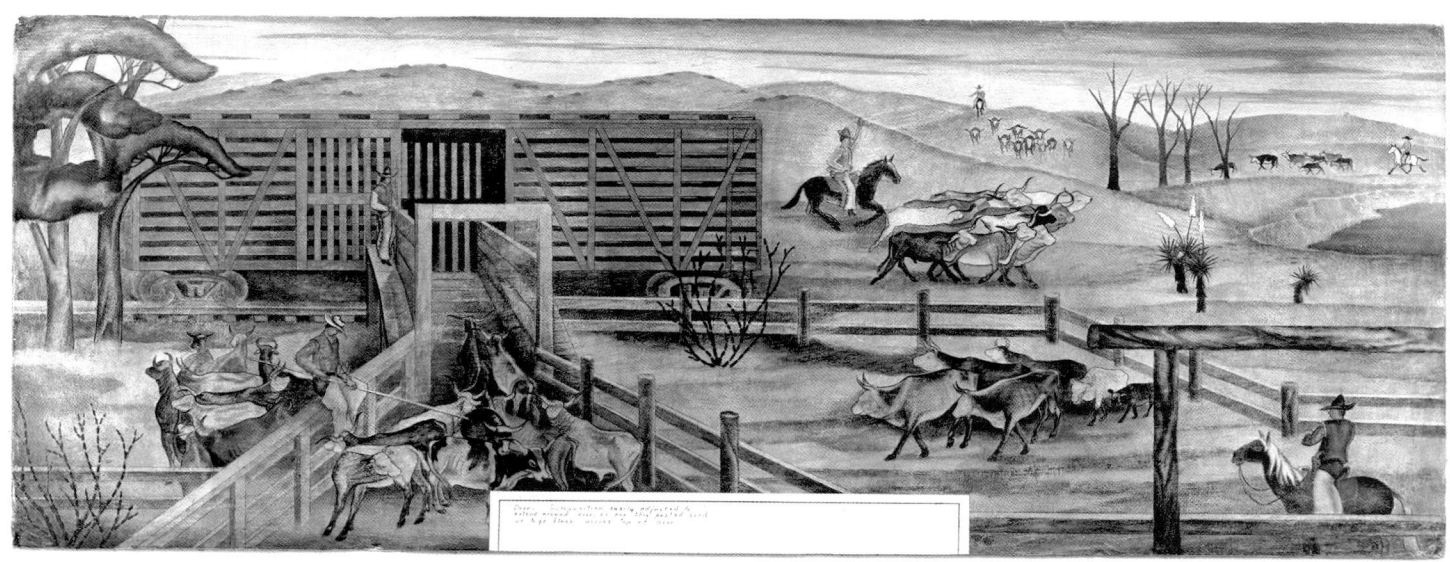

48 STATES COMP.

Musick's study, one of two submitted in the 48 States
Competition, was posed for the Red Cloud post office.
Musick favored the subject, although the town was not
historically noted for longhorn cattle drives.

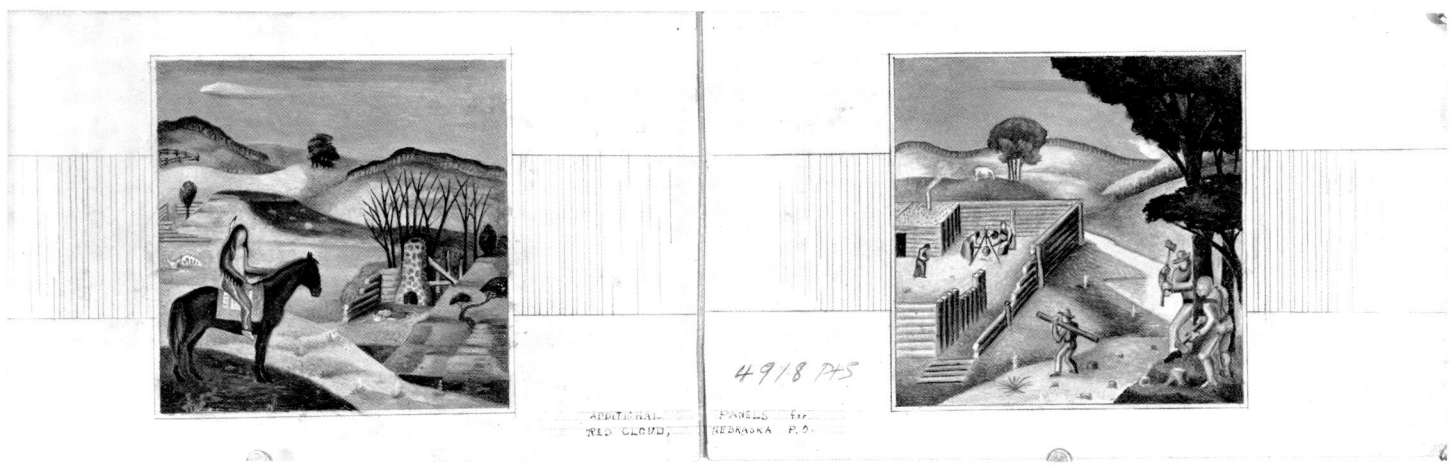

Musick went through several refinements for his two murals entitled *Moving Westward* and *Stockade Builders*, beginning first with these black-and-white studies.

Section. He had completed his first mural in 1934 under the Public Works of Art Project, but for years received little notice from the Section. "I have to hold myself back to keep from gushing over," he wrote. "When one has been stalked by a nemesis for six straight years, such good news comes to him something in the form of a haymaker."[67]

After taking his Wyoming subjects to Red Cloud, Musick reported that one design would be appropriate. "I am glad to say that the cattle loading one definitely is. Hundreds of tons of beef traversed that valley, even Texas longhorns."[68] In fact, Red Cloud was not known to have been a shipping point for Texas longhorn cattle. Musick may have been mistaken about local history, or may simply have desired to use the subject at hand.

The local postmaster, however, had other ideas. "[H]e and the majority of the townspeople sort of had their heart set on some reference to Chief Red Cloud, for whom the town was named," Musick wrote. However, the postmaster said, "But of course we'll take what we can get." The outspoken artist objected to the local preference by citing an *Omaha World-Herald* article that said Red Cloud had massacred whites, established a "military dictatorship," and was "crafty" and "treacherous." Musick wrote to Rowan, "I don't see any point in glorifying him, even from the viewpoint of the citizens."[69]

In the end, Musick promised to take the community's preference to the Section. And Solomon-like, Rowan found an unobligated balance in the building's construction fund to add $500 to the artist's $800 contract. This paid for two additional panels on the screen wall above the postal clerks' counters — one of which would include a depiction of Chief Red Cloud. Musick replied, "I wish to say that being 'agreeable with this proposal' is indeed a very mild way of putting it . . . And I am happy at this solution whereby the citizens of Red Cloud won't accept their mural with a grudge."[70] Because of Rowan's compromise, Red Cloud was the only Nebraska post office to receive three murals.

The artist still expressed discouragement when he sent black-and-white sketches for the two additional panels. "I realize it will be a problem to raise this portrait of Red Cloud (on

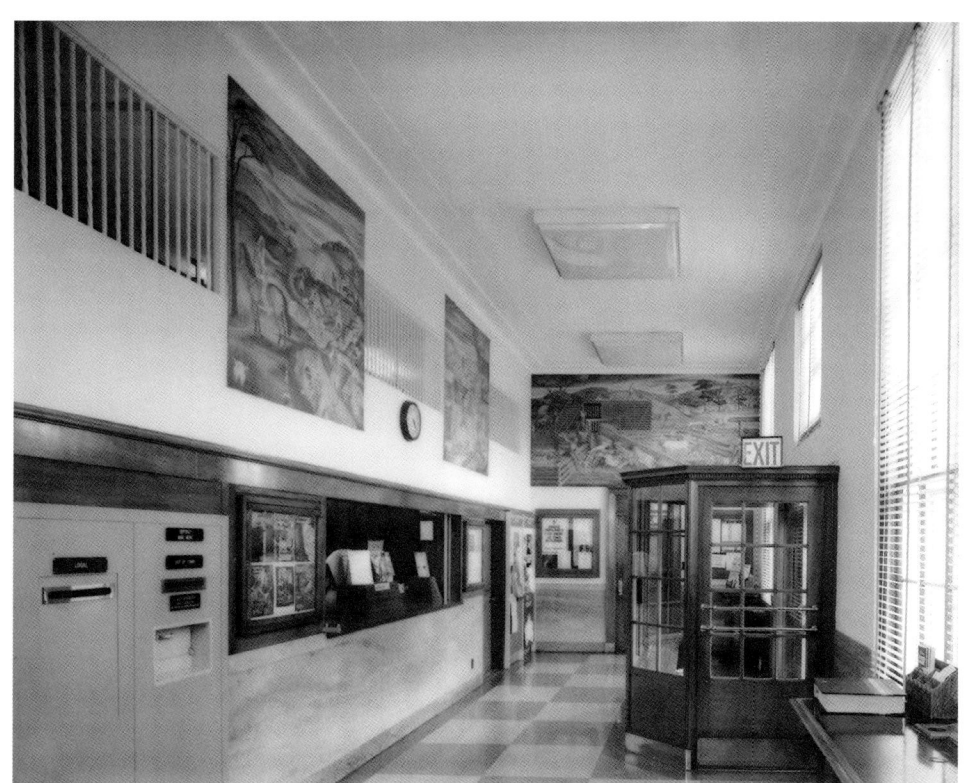

Interior of the Red Cloud post office. It is the only Nebraska commission to include three murals, shown here with two panels above the postal clerks' counters and the third at the typical placement above the postmaster's door.

the horse) above the commonplace . . . Besides [William] Gropper I can't think of anyone off hand who has done murals without the utilization of heroic figures. But I think it is worth attempting and since I started that way with the cattle loading scene, I'm keeping these in the same scale and mood."[71]

The Section's comments on the black-and-white studies may reveal the artist's lingering reluctance regarding the subject matter. Rowan wrote, "Frankly, the new designs do not seem to carry the same sense of inspiration that characterized the cattle-loading panel . . . I realize that the medium of black and white paint which you have used for these murals is not very inspired and as you have handled it would tend to detract from even more exciting designs." Rowan asked for further sketches. Musick replied, "It was my intention to emphasize a certain feeling of destruction and loneliness in this panel by leaving out all life except the horseman [Red Cloud] who . . . sadly contemplates the destruction wrought by him and his men and its impotence in the face of the busy stockade builders and the teeming cattle industry."[72]

Musick submitted two new pencil renderings of the panels, but Rowan criticized these as well, this time focusing on the scale of the figures. Musick proposed to go ahead with color sketches "hoping against hope that you will approve them." In describing how he paired the two murals, he wrote, "I've tried to compose the two designs, together with the space between, as a complete unit." He was authorized to proceed, Rowan saying only that they were "satisfactory."[73]

The criticism continued with the color sketches. Rowan said the figure on horseback "does not convincingly sit on the horse. It is also suggested that the figures at work be made more convincingly functional. Take the man who is cutting down the tree. Make him where he would normally be during such an act."[74] Musick was, however, authorized to proceed with the full-size cartoon, garnering his first payment.

After completion (but before installation) one of the murals received a final criticism from the Section, based upon the black-and-white photographs Musick submitted. Rowan wrote, "[T]he trees on the right of the woodchopping panel are confusing in black and white. It is as though another level and a deeper plane were introduced in the trunks above

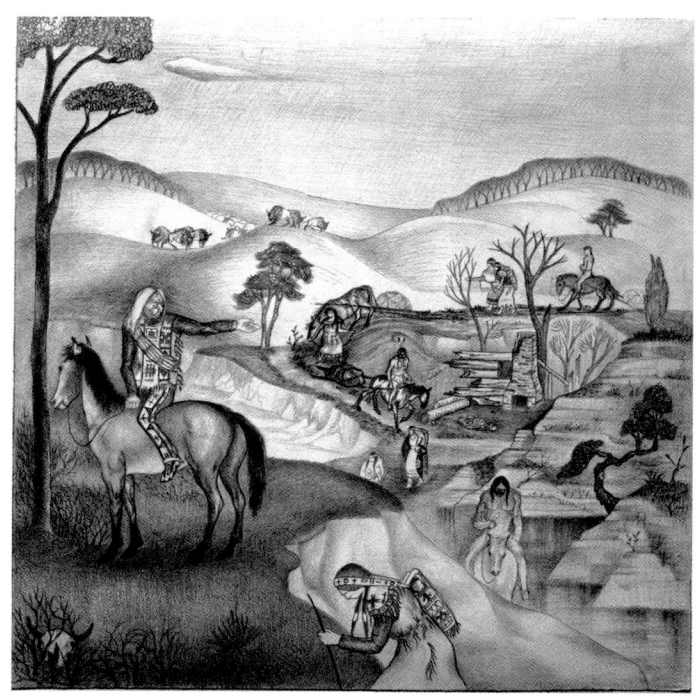

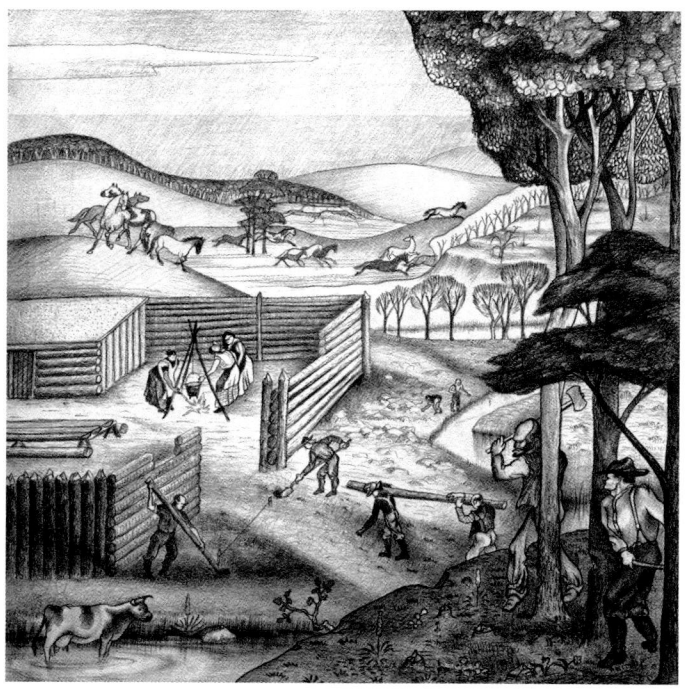

Musick added a procession of Native Americans to his subsequent submittal, probably intending to enhance the feeling of their dispossession.

For another study of the mural, *Stockade Builders*, Musick was asked to make the figures at work "convincingly functional."

the foliage occurring on the central line of the composition."[75] Although rarely done, Rowan even prepared a small tracing showing the suggested change. Musick, however, proceeded with installation in April 1941. Having noted Rowan's comments, he blamed the quality of the photographs he submitted. With so many detailed comments from Rowan, it had taken Musick almost sixteen months to complete the project.

The postmaster forwarded comments on the completed mural: "There is varied comment on the work. The younger people are critical as they consider the conditions portrayed in the pictures could not have existed even in pioneer days. The older people consider it typical of early day conditions." But the local newspaper reacted favorably: "These pioneer scenes are vividly done and are attracting much attention and comment."[76]

BORN IN MISSOURI, Archie Musick studied journalism and briefly went into that profession, but eventually chose art. In his early years he traveled extensively in a robust lifestyle. Regarding his first murals, Musick recalled them as "scenic pot-boilers on restaurant walls, [which] were happily destroyed by fire."[77] Early in his career, he studied with Randall Davey and Ernest Lawson at the Broadmoor Art Academy in Colorado Springs. He then studied at the Art Students League in New York under Thomas Hart Benton, and then in California under Stanton Macdonald-Wright. He participated in the Public Works of Art Project, completing a mural for the city auditorium in Colorado Springs. Returning to the former Broadmoor Art Academy, now renamed the Colorado Springs Fine Arts Center, he studied under Boardman Robinson. His classmates included Jenne and Ethel Magafan, Edward Chavez, and others who were then engaged in Section murals. His only other commission for the Section was for the Manitou Springs, Colorado, post office. He taught variously over the next years at the Cheyenne Mountain (Colorado) High School, University of Missouri, Columbia (Missouri) College, and the University of Colorado at Colorado Springs.

Philip von Saltza (1885–1980) | *Wild Horses by Moonlight*

1940, OIL ON CANVAS

This mural depicts two rearing wild horses in the foreground, frightened by a coiled rattle-snake. The horses are firmly grounded above the postmaster's door. The moonlit sky and dark nighttime colors add to the scene's intense mood. The Section was pleased with the "color and the emotional qualities of the painting." A contemporary biographer of von Saltza described his post office murals as "like Gershwin tunes of the thirties. They are broad stroked, somewhat ethereal and impressionistic."[78]

Philip von Saltza entered his design for *Wild Horses by Moonlight* for Safford, Arizona, in the 48 States Competition — one of several he submitted for various post offices. But in the competition's checkerboard game of switching designs from one state to another, the submittal was instead selected for Schuyler, Nebraska, earning the artist a $740 commission. When the picture of von Saltza's mural study appeared in *Life* magazine, the local newspaper criticized the work in a folksy editorial: "But my gorsh, here in Schuyler we're to have 'wild horses in a cactus field.' Very typical of this section of the United States, don't you think?" Noting that the photo caption in the *Life* article promised that the cactus would be changed to "tall poplar trees," the newspaper editor remained skeptical, and consulted an old time local resident: "That wild horse business sort of got to us and we went out

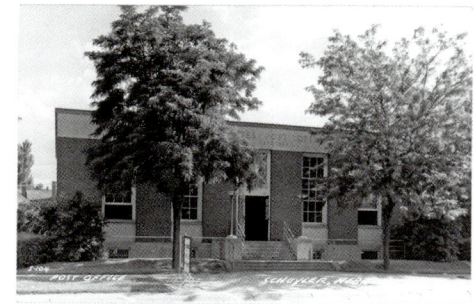

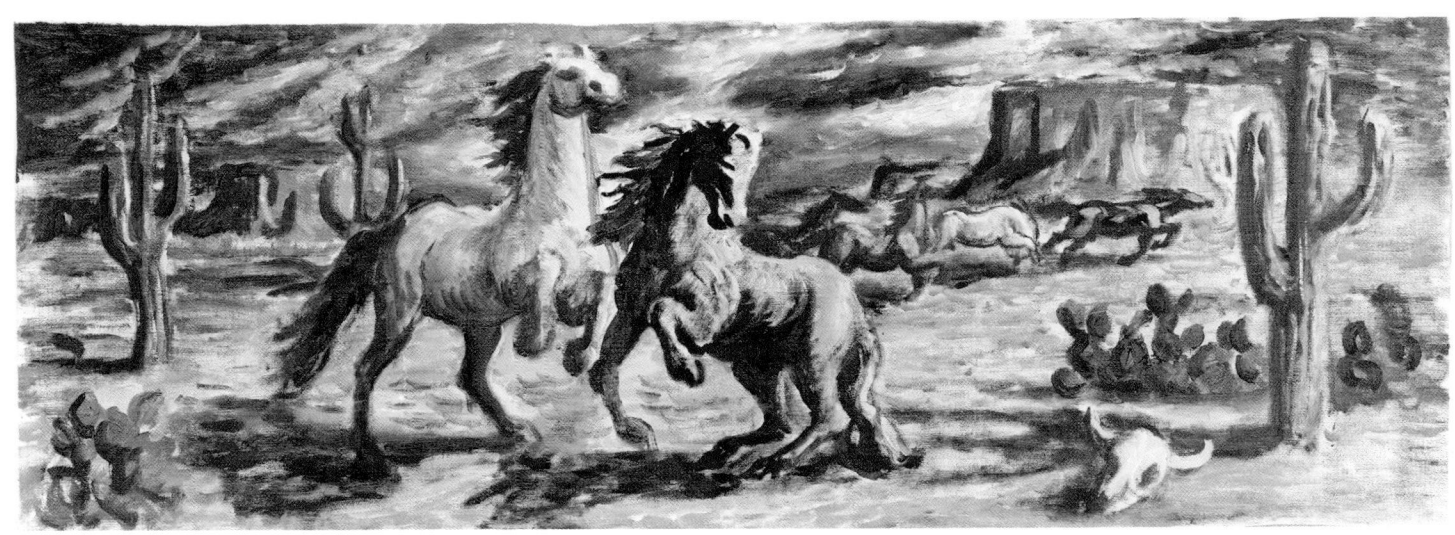

Intended for an Arizona post office, von Saltza's
entry in the 48 States Competition included
desert mesas and cacti.

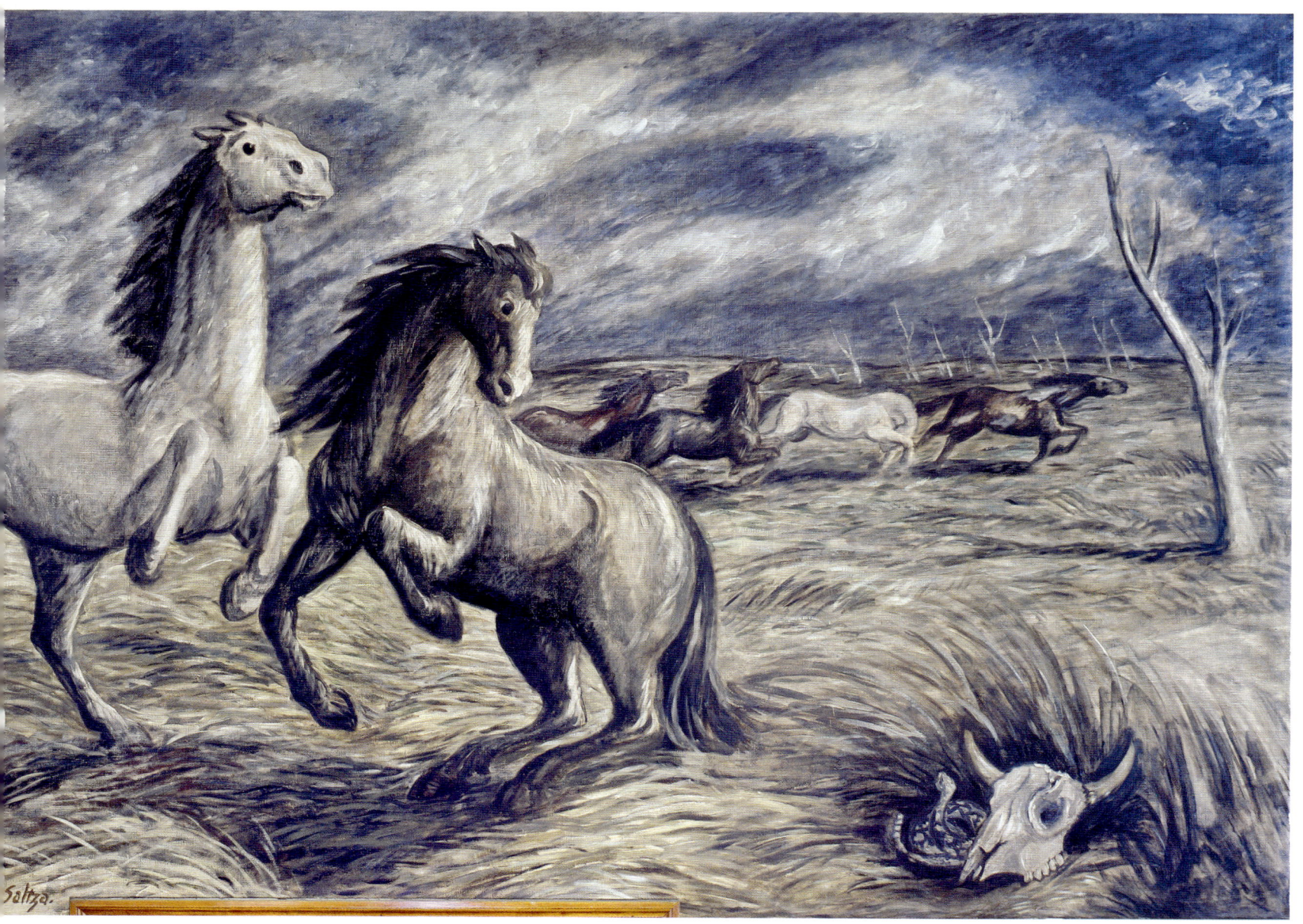

PLATE 11

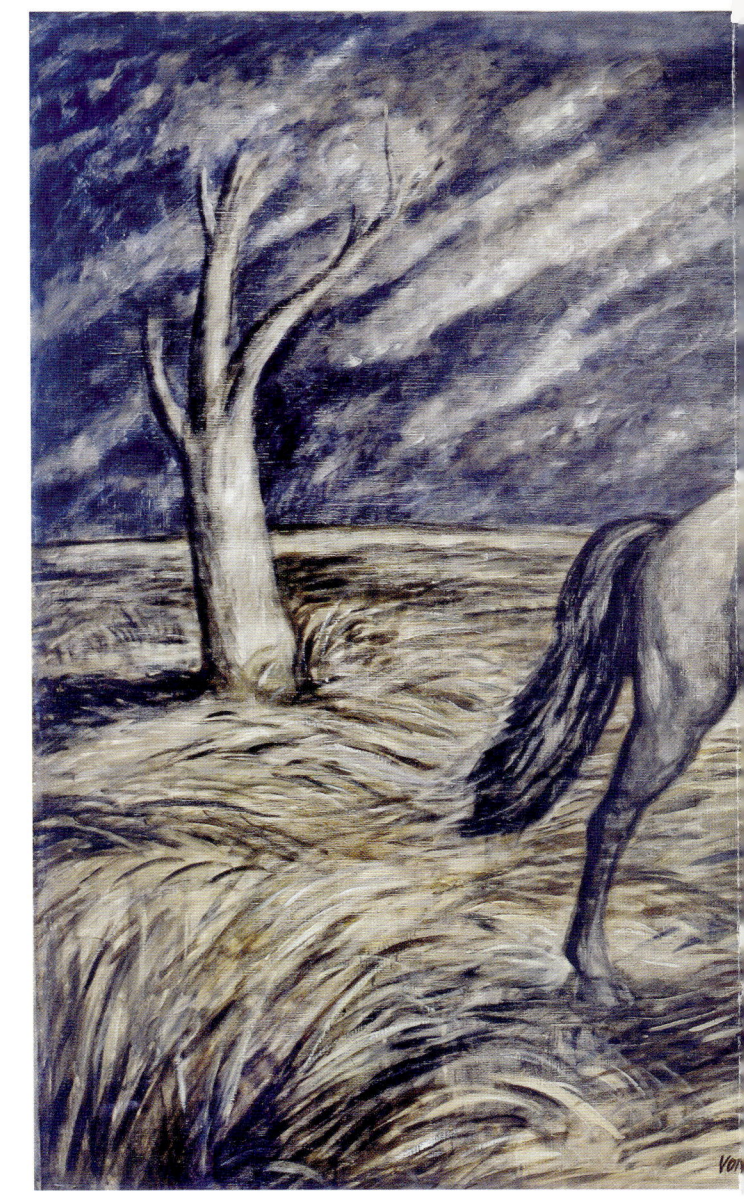

to ask if wild horses roamed this section in the early days. The gentleman we questioned said 'sure, why in the early days you could even buy wild horse meat in a local butcher shop.'" Referring to another artist's unsuccessful entry, which included oxen, the editor said, "Oxen, to our way of thinking, were tops over wild horses here in the early days."[79]

Von Saltza's next task was to delete the desert mesas and, at Rowan's suggestion, turn the cacti into "poplar" trees, probably a reference to native cottonwoods. Rowan wrote:

> [Q]uestion was raised relative to the landscape, which will need restudy in order to make it appropriate to and reflective of the locale. On a trip through Nebraska this past summer I was impressed by certain poplar trees which had been polished like fine silver by the sand carried in the winds. In many instances the tops of the trees were completely gone and they stood like stark candelabra in the landscape.
>
> Cacti are not a usual element in the Nebraska landscape, as well you know. I mention the trees . . . thinking that you might be able to introduce one or two of those to replace the cacti in your design although I think it will also be necessary to show a little more lush quality in the landscape in order to make the work acceptable to the public.[80]

Rowan asked von Saltza to submit a black-and-white scale sketch after further research, and after approving that, told the artist to proceed with the full-size cartoon. Receiving a photograph of the cartoon, Rowan was pleased: "[Y]ou have introduced a good deal of vitality into the work. It seems distinctly American."[81]

After the mural was installed, the Schuyler postmistress wrote that the "picture has attracted a great deal of attention and much favorable comment . . . it is really very beautiful and striking. . . It is very interesting to watch the public, young and old, stop to admire the picture and voice their opinions. Mr. von Saltza would be very happy to hear their comments." She said the mural was a subject of study by the local Women's Club, resulting in some "very interesting discussions."[82]

However, the postmistress also noted that "we are not without our critics. The severest not to say the most competent critic thinks he [von Saltza] modeled his horses after the 'Merry-go-round,' and that one horse really has his neck stuck out." Having met the artist, who traveled to Schuyler to install the mural, she added, "We are glad this particular artist won the award, as we were very favorably impressed with not only the artist but the man himself. He was so human and understanding."[83]

PHILIP VON SALTZA WAS born in Stockholm, Sweden, and emigrated to the United States with his family in 1891 at the age of six. His father was a genre painter and illustrator; in the United States he took up portrait painting and encouraged his son to begin painting at an early age. At age fourteen, von Saltza entered Columbia University and graduated with an engineer of mines degree, practicing in Arizona and Colorado, where he also painted. After returning to New York City, he left engineering for an art career, studying at the Art Students League in New York City. He was a veteran both of the Mexican border skirmishes and World War I, being wounded and taken a prisoner of war. He practiced in New England. His work was exhibited at the 1939 New York World's Fair.

Besides the mural study that was taken to Schuyler, another entry by von Saltza in the 48 States Competition led to a mural at the post office in Milford, New Hampshire. He also completed murals for the Section in Williamston, North Carolina, and two for the Saint Albans, Vermont, post office. In addition to practicing his art, he went on to be an antiques dealer and furniture restorer.

Kady Faulkner (1901–77) | *End of the Line*

1939, OIL AND EGG TEMPERA ON CANVAS

During her early years, Kady Faulkner's typical approach was a realistic type of genre painting, applying a regionalist formula and a distinct sense of color and texture. Her mural for the Valentine post office is an example of this approach. Leonard Thiessen, artist and art critic for the *Omaha World-Herald*, said the "strong point . . . is the clear, virile color, sometimes obtained by painting green hills over red under-painting to obtain a sort of stop-and-go vibration."[84]

Faulkner also found a way to carry her mural to the tops of the bulletin boards. Here she incorporates two vignettes flanking the postmaster's door, referred to as predella. Both are Sandhills scenes — one of open range, the other of barbed-wire fences and windmills. Each is broken above by a dark band incorporating actual cattle brands of local ranches, a feature that Rowan found "very interesting."[85]

Faulkner had entered a 1938 regional competition for the post office terminal annex building in Dallas, Texas. The competition was open to artists in seventeen states, and runners-up were to be invited to submit designs for fifteen other smaller post offices, including Valentine. The Section later announced that due to the large number of quality entries (152 artists in all) it was expanding the number of participating post offices to thirty.[86]

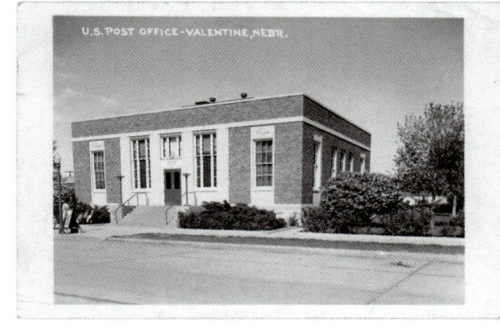

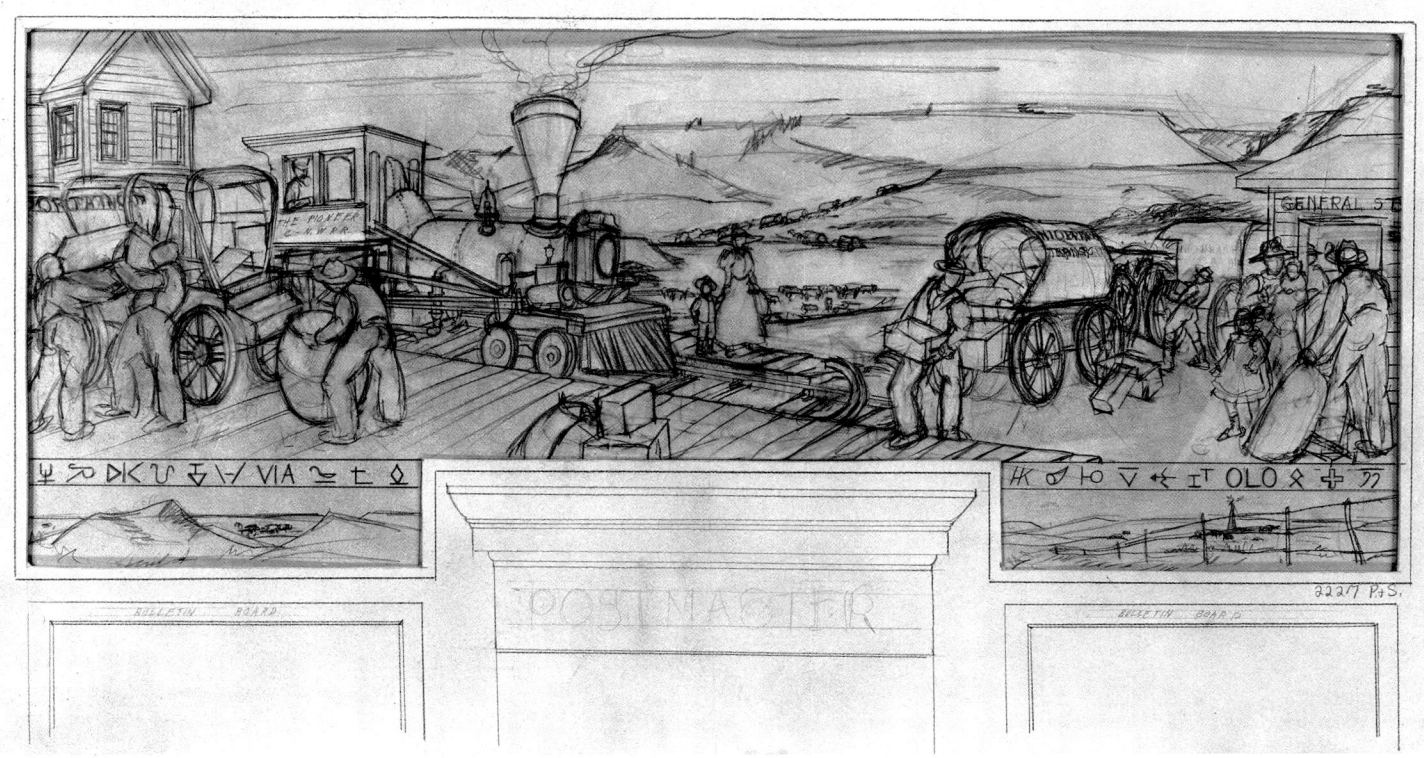

Faulkner's first pencil sketch for the Valentine mural.

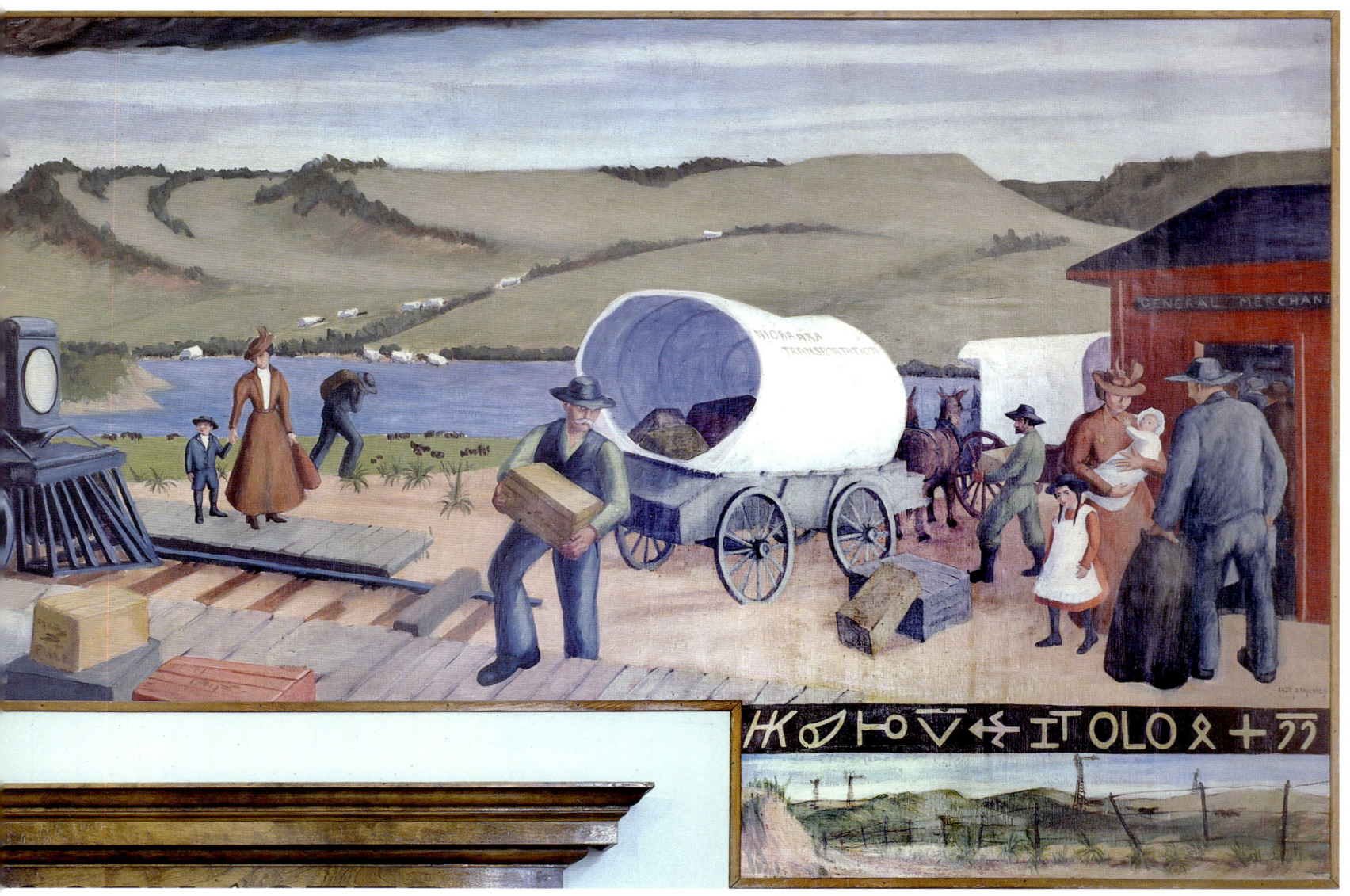

PLATE 12

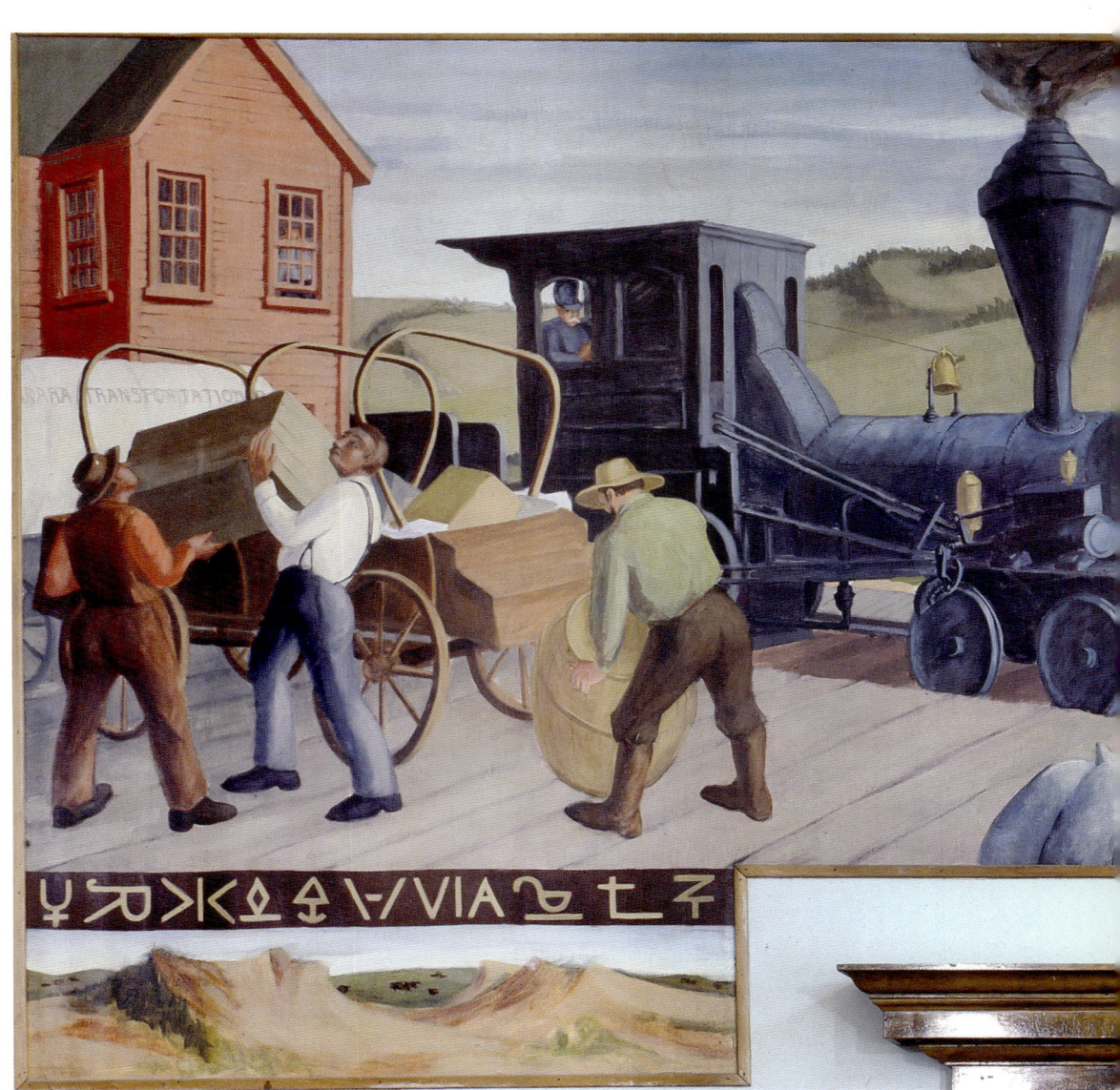

Faulkner was awarded a $620 commission and received a letter from Rowan telling her "how much I personally liked your designs." Soon afterward she traveled to Valentine to observe local landscapes and glean information about the town. Accompanied by the postmistress, she viewed scenery along the Niobrara River.[87] She selected an historical theme entitled *End of the Line*, representing both the coming of the railroad to the new town and the freighting company that once served the area.

"We regard the subject matter as unusual and interesting and I am confident that you will be able to create a really handsome decoration," Rowan wrote when the Section approved the black-and-white sketch. "The only suggestion that is offered relative to your design is that the figures in the foreground on the extreme right and left do not be crowded against the enframement. We feel it would be much better to bring them slightly more into the composition."[88]

Faulkner next submitted a color sketch, to which Rowan replied, "The only suggestion offered is that the band of symbols between the main panel and the predella may be too low in value. I refer particularly to the background color of this band."[89] After that, the Section accepted her full-size cartoon, and she completed the mural four months later.

Although the Section lauded Faulkner's work, her mural was the most controversial of any painted in Nebraska and was poorly received by local newspapers. The Valentine *Republican* was especially harsh in its criticism of the mural's portrayal of local scenery:

In the background are some treeless hills. If they are considered the hills of the Minnekadusa [creek] north of town, then the train has come in from the west, whereas the railroad of course was built from the east. If they are the hills of the Niobrara canyon . . . then the depot is on the wrong side of the tracks. Each of these hills was thickly studded with native pine, and not treeless. . . This paper had expected to reproduce a picture of the painting but under the circumstances has decided to refrain from irritating its readers to that extent.[90]

The *Republican* also found fault with historical details. "Should a mural painting in a public building be allegorical or historical?" it asked rhetorically, complaining that the covered wagon's canvas top was in the shape of a "roll," and that the locomotive was "a

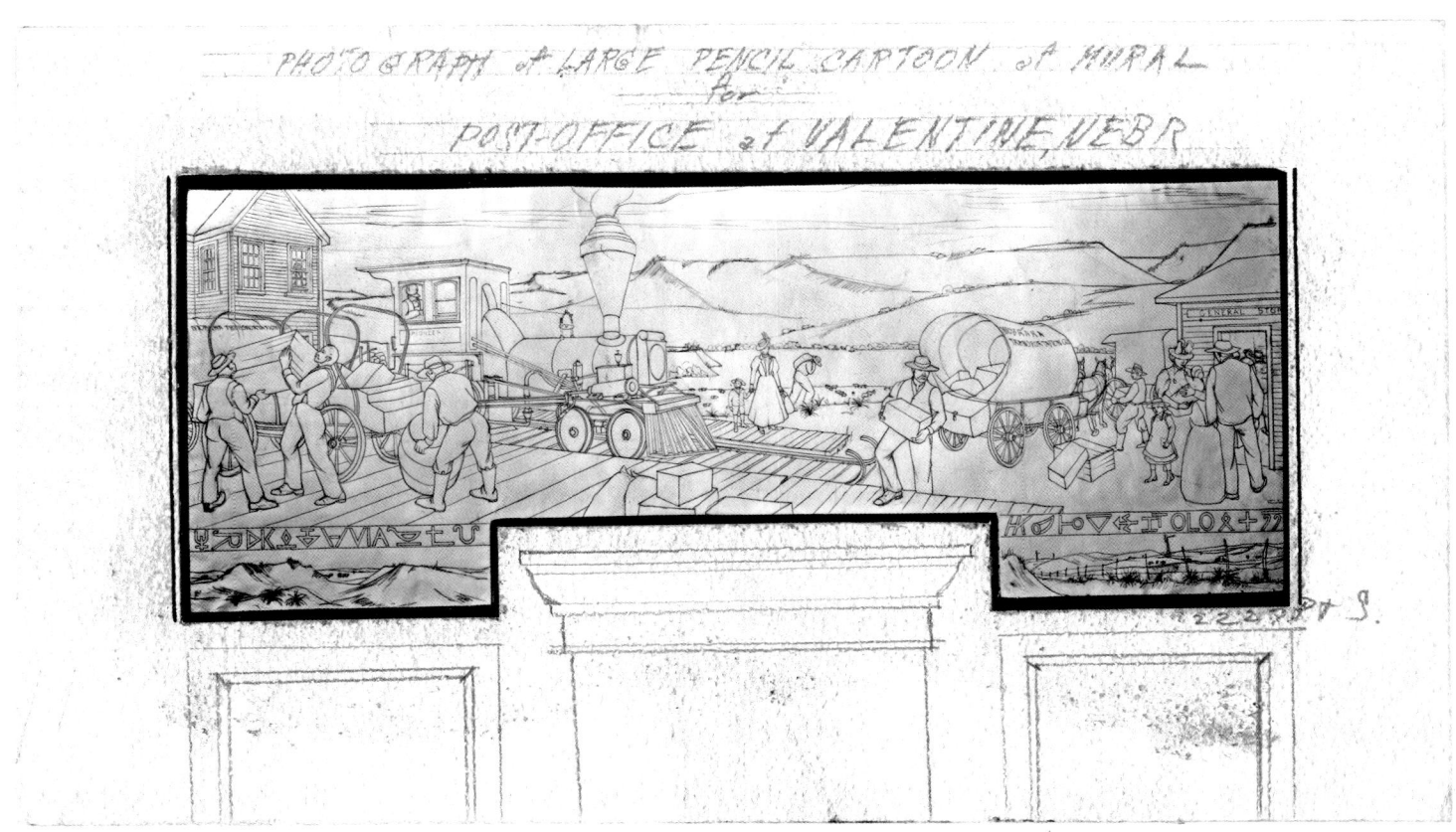

A photograph of the full-size cartoon for the Valentine Post Office. Faulkner changed the composition of the figures to the right and left to satisfy Rowan, who cautioned that they not be "crowded against the enframement."

toy affair" of the wrong vintage, although supposedly based on information provided by the head office of a railroad company in Chicago.[91]

The *Cherry County News* joined in: "We hope those early day residents possessed neither faces nor feet such as are pictured and two men holding a large box are said to have a life time job. We understand the cost of this painting is probably about $700 and are glad the investment is not ours."[92]

After the *Nebraska State Journal* published Faulkner's defense, the Valentine *Republican* said she "admitted that perhaps the locomotive was not quite of the proper date, but that if she had painted a larger boiler it would obscure some of the details she wanted in the background! This statement indicates that artists do not give much importance to truth in detail. Probably discussion is useless, as we shall have to take the mural as it exists, and not as we think it should be." And in the same spirit of grudging acceptance, the *Republican* said at the time of the mural's installation that it "will never add to the 'gayety of the nations,' but it has already added much to the gayety of Valentine, and will doubtless continue to do so."[93]

Criticism of the mural pitted the local press against the statewide newspapers. The *Lincoln Star, Nebraska State Journal,* and *Omaha World-Herald* all voiced support for Faulkner's work. A *State Journal* editorial said that Faulkner's "effort was to portray vividly a pioneer scene. As the picture is merely interpretive, it was not deemed necessary to make it conform in every detail to the local scene. It was regional rather than local." The editorial concluded that the "home folks" were "more irritated because they have concluded that 'the dictators at Washington will decide.'"[94]

Under the headline, "Art Storm . . . Over Valentine," the *Omaha World-Herald* reported that Faulkner didn't seem particularly upset, and that she said the local press was judging the work only by a newspaper photograph. "Some of her critics, she thinks, may have a change of heart when they see the completed work." Dr. Lester Longman, head of the University of Iowa art department, spoke before the Nebraska Art Association in Lincoln, where he viewed the completed work. He, too, defended the artist: "Leonardo da Vinci didn't have a ticket to the last supper . . . but he painted a masterpiece of the event." Rowan replied to Longman, "I appreciated particularly your very convincing argument in commenting on the criticism which has been given to Miss Kady Faulkner's mural . . . It was extremely kind of you to champion this able and sincere artist."[95]

To explain her work, which by then had been installed, Faulkner traveled to Valentine and at the invitation of the local postmistress gave a presentation to a group of about fifty women of the community. Faulkner reported that "their response was quite heartening."[96] In a letter to Rowan, the postmistress explained the community's reaction:

It has been under fire of the editors of our local newspapers. I understand that the art critics think it a fine piece of work. I believe if the sketch had been submitted to a local pioneer committee, before it was accepted it would have insured its popularity. Communities are so touchy about their local history.

Miss Faulkner had marvelous subject material at hand on which to base a theme but she was not acquainted with our country and painted what any one from the east would like.[97]

Rowan replied with support for Faulkner, calling her work "distinguished" and a "commendable decoration," adding that it "was the intention of this office . . . to have the work executed by a person living and working in Nebraska and hence acquainted with the state in a way that an outsider could not have been."[98]

Rowan also wrote Faulkner, saying "[I] very much regret that you have run up against this type of criticism. I wish to congratulate you on the dignified stand which the newspaper clippings indicate you have taken."[99]

Although the Section attempted to select local talent whenever possible, Faulkner was the only Nebraska artist to win a commission for a post office in her home state. The Valentine mural was her only work for the Section.

BORN IN SYRACUSE, NEW YORK, Katherine "Kady" Faulkner attended Syracuse University from 1921 to 1925, earning a BFA (later earning an MA from that institution in 1938). She also studied at the Art Students League in New York under Boardman Robinson, Henry Varnum Poor, and Hans Hofmann. After several teaching positions, Faulkner joined the University of Nebraska art department in 1930, eventually serving a twenty-year tenure. A dedicated but demanding teacher, she believed that teaching should come before creative work. She explained her concept of art in a 1937 interview: "Modern art merely translates the experiences we have in everyday life by light, space, color, lines and forms. It is simply an application of creative living."[100] Faulkner left Nebraska in 1950 after disagreements at the university. She settled in Kenosha, Wisconsin, where she served as head of the art department at Kemper Hall, an Episcopalian boarding school for girls. She retired in 1972. Her style evolved from the realistic to the abstract, and she worked in oils, watercolor, and tempera, and made etchings and silk screen prints.

Acknowledgments

AS THESE PAGES SHOW, the National Archives contains valuable materials and information pertaining to the post office mural project. The staff there assisted in locating photographs of pencil sketches, scale drawings, and cartoons, as well as items from the meticulous correspondence between artists and Treasury officials. Access to these resources allowed me to represent the evolution of each work from preliminary sketch to mural, with generous notations and critiques between artists and the Section.

Correspondence with Jenne Currie, daughter of Ethel Magafan and niece of Jenne Magafan, provided much helpful information about these remarkable sisters. Likewise, correspondence with Michael Mechau, son of Frank Mechau, revealed much about this talented artist. Both are keepers of the great heritage of these artists. I thoroughly appreciate their contributions to this work.

I also wish to thank colleagues David Bristow, associate director for publications, and John Carter, senior research folklorist, for their encouragement throughout production. Pat Gaster, assistant editor, prepared the index and Cindy Drake, library curator, processed many interlibrary loan forms in the course of the research. Michael J. Smith, director/CEO of the Nebraska State Historical Society, supported this work throughout. Also deserving thanks for their encouragement were those represented on the publications committee of the Nebraska State Historical Society, including Jim McKee. I am proud that this book will be among the many recognized publications by the historical society.

Photographer John Nollendorfs of Lincoln, Nebraska, provided high-quality scans of Jeffrey Beebe's mural photographs. Joy Carey, NSHS editorial assistant, did much of the Photoshop work to prepare the other images for publication.

Finally, I express gratitude to James C. and Rhonda Seacrest for underwriting the publication of this book. The Seacrests are known for their immense support for the arts in Nebraska, and it is an honor to have this book recognized by their generous contribution.

Notes

Mural Art in the New Deal

1 Frederick P. Keppel and R. L. Duffus, *The Arts in American Life* (New York and London: McGraw-Hill Book Company, 1933), 122, 202.

2 Acceptance speech before the Democratic National Convention, Chicago, July 2, 1932, Franklin D. Roosevelt Presidential Library and Museum.

3 George Biddle, "An Art Renaissance under Federal Patronage," *Scribner's Magazine* 95 (June 1934): 428.

4 "cw Artists," *Time*, December 25, 1933, 19.

5 As quoted in Karal Ann Marling, *Wall-to-Wall America* (Minneapolis: University of Minnesota Press, 1982), 42.

6 "cw Artists."

7 Edward Bruce and Forbes Watson, *Art in Federal Buildings, Volume I* (Washington, D.C.: Art in Federal Buildings Inc., 1936), 284.

8 Ibid.

9 As quoted in Matthew Baigell, *The American Scene: American Painting of the 1930's* (New York and Washington: Praeger Publishers, Inc. 1974), 18.

10 "It's All Very Confusing, This Selection of Art," *Des Moines* (Sunday) *Register*, April 29, 1934, 7:11.

11 Edward Bruce in Bruce and Watson, *Art in Federal Buildings*, 284.

12 "Government Inspiration," *Time*, March 2, 1936, 43; Virginia Mecklenburg, *The Public as Patron* (College Park, MD. University of Maryland, 1979), 10; Marling, *Wall-to Wall America*, 43; Bruce and Watson, *Art in Federal Buildings*, 284.

13 As quoted in Marlene Park and Gerald E. Markowitz, *Democratic Vistas: Post Offices and Public Art in the New Deal* (Philadelphia: Temple University Press, 1984), 31; Mecklenburg, *The Public as Patron*, 10, as quoted from an article by George Biddle in *American Magazine of Art*, September 1934; "First All-Nebraska Mural for Valentine Post Office," *Omaha* (Sunday) *World-Herald*, February 26, 1939, c:8.

14 Ernest F. Witte, "The Nebraska FERA Art Exhibit," *Nebraska History* 16, no. 1 (January-March 1935): 57.

15 "It's All Very Confusing;" "A Little Dispute, Yes; But Dignified," *Omaha* (Sunday) *World-Herald*, April 29, 1934, Section A:8.

16 "Omaha Artist Paints Twin 'Old Man River,'" *Omaha* (Sunday) *Bee-News*, April 29, 1934, Section A:2.

17 Ibid.

18 "A Little Dispute"; "Omaha Artist Paints Twin 'Old Man River'"; "It's All Very Confusing."

19 Nebraska State Historical Society collections inventory.

20 Witte, "The Nebraska FERA Art Exhibit," 57.

21 Ibid., 59.

22 William F. McDonald, *Federal Relief Administration and the Arts* (Columbus: Ohio State University Press, 1969), 385.

23 Belisario R. Contreras, *Tradition and Innovation in New Deal Art* (London and Toronto: Associated University Presses, 1983), 142.

24 *Bulletin Number 1* (Section of Painting and Sculpture, March 1, 1935), 5.

25 *Bulletin Number 5* (Section of Painting and Sculpture, September 1935), 8.

26 Richard D. McKinzie, *The New Deal for Artists* (Princeton, N.J.: Princeton University Press, 1973), 37.

27 Bruce and Watson, *Art in Federal Buildings*, 286.

28 *Bulletin Number 5*, 8.

29 "Government Artists' Work on Display at Joslyn Memorial...," *Omaha* (Sunday) *World-Herald*, May 24, 1936, 7E.

30 Augustus W. Dunbier to Olin Dows, August 16, 1935, and Dwight Kirsch to Olin Dows, August 25, 1935, Archives of American Art, Smithsonian Institution, RG 121, microfilm reel DC29 (Nebraska).

31 Ibid., Olin Dows to Dwight Kirsch, August 29, 1935; Dwight Kirsch to Olin Dows, October 14, 1935; Olin Dows to Dwight Kirsch, October 21, 1935.

32 "Government Inspiration."

33 *Annual Report of the Secretary of the Treasury on the State of the Finances for the Fiscal Year Ended June 30, 1937* (Washington, D.C.: Government Printing Office, 1938), 188; McKinzie, *The New Deal for Artists*, 39, 42.

34 Edward Bruce in Bruce and Watson, *Art in Federal Buildings*, 284; *Bulletin Number 5*, 3.

35 Edward Bruce in Bruce and Watson, *Art in Federal Buildings*, 284.

36 *Bulletin Number 5*, 3.

37 *Bulletin Number 1*, 3–4.

38 Philip Evergood, "Concerning Mural Painting," in Francis V. O'Connor, ed., *Art for the Millions* (Boston: New York Graphic Society, 1975), 48.

39 Edward Bruce in Bruce and Watson, *Art in Federal Buildings*, 289; *Bulletin 19* (Section of Fine Arts, June 1939), 3.

40 Edward Bruce in Bruce and Watson, *Art in Federal Buildings*, 285.

41 Forbes Watson in Bruce and Watson, *Art in Federal Buildings*, 23–24.

42 *History of Post Office Construction, 1900–1940* (United States Postal Service, Office of Real Estate, July 1982), 14.

43 *Bulletin Number 5*, 5.

44 As quoted in Park and Markowitz, *Democratic Vistas*, 8; as quoted in Mecklenburg, *The Public as Patron*, 14.

45 Park and Markowitz, *Democratic Vistas*, 69, 138; McKinzie, *The New Deal for Artists*, 55.

46 Oral interview with Kenneth Evett, October 10, 1964, Archives of American Art, Smithsonian Institution, RG121, microfilm reel DC29 (Nebraska).

47 *Annual Report of the Secretary of the Treasury on the State of the Finances for the Fiscal Year Ended June 30, 1938* (Washington, D.C.: Government Printing Office, 1939), 201; Park and Markowitz, *Democratic Vistas*, 12; *Bulletin Number 5*, 6.

48 McKinzie, *The New Deal for Artists*, 54; *Bulletin Number 1*, 5.

49 *Bulletin Number 9* (Section of Painting and Sculpture, March, April, May 1936), 9.

50 *Bulletin Number 1*, 4.

51 *Bulletin Number 9*, 11; Park and Markowitz, *Democratic Vistas*, 12–13. Some artists received more than one commission.

52 Oral interview with Kenneth Evett, October 10, 1964; Park and Markowitz, *Democratic Vistas*, 8.

53 Archie Musick to Edward B. Rowan, January 15, 1940, National Archives, RG 121, Entry 133, Box 61 (hereafter National Archives), Red Cloud Post Office file.

54 Mary Pollard Hull, "Designs for Mural Paintings Shown at Joslyn Memorial," *Omaha* (Sunday) *World-Herald*, June 13, 1937, 11E.

55 "Gentle Hogarth," *Time*, July 26, 1937, 46.

56 *Annual Report of the Secretary of the Treasury on the State of the Finances for the Fiscal Year Ended June 30, 1915* (Washington, D.C.: Government Printing Office, 1916), 30–31.

57 *History of Post Office Construction*, 17.

58 Ibid., 29; "Crawford May Get Building," *Lincoln Star*, June 18, 1937, 14.

59 *History of Post Office Construction*, 16; "P.O. Projects for Five Towns," *Omaha Bee-News*, November 11, 1933, 2.

60 *Annual Report of the Secretary of the Treasury on the State of the Finances for the Fiscal Year Ended June 30, 1937*, 182.

61 Edward Bruce in Bruce and Watson, *Art in Federal Buildings,* 284.

62 As quoted in Park and Markowitz, *Democratic Vistas,* 114.

63 *Bulletin Number 8* (Section of Painting and Sculpture, January-February 1936), 14.

64 Hull, "Designs for Mural Paintings Shown at Joslyn Memorial."

65 Edward B. Rowan to G. Glenn Newell, April 5, 1940, National Archives, Crawford Post Office file.

66 Hull, "Designs for Mural Paintings Shown at Joslyn Memorial;" *Bulletin Number 4* (Section of Painting and Sculpture, July-August 1935), 6.

67 As quoted in Park and Markowitz, *Democratic Vistas,* 116.

68 Marling, *Wall-to-Wall America,* 51; Archie Musick, *Musick Medley* (Colorado Springs: Creative Press Adv., Inc., September 1971), 90.

69 "First All-Nebraska Mural for Valentine Postoffice."

70 Edward B. Rowan to Frank Mechau, September 13, 1938, National Archives, Ogallala Post Office file.

71 Carl Eric Linden to Edward B. Rowan, March 5, 1940, National Archives, Ogallala Post Office file; Edward B. Rowan to Frank Mechau, September 13, 1938; Park and Markowitz, *Democratic Vistas,* 116.

72 Edward B. Rowan to Frank Mechau, September 13, 1938, National Archives, Ogallala Post Office file.

73 Edward B. Rowan to Eugene Trentham, October 27, 1937, National Archives, O'Neill Post Office file; William E. L. Bunn to Edward B. Rowan, September 22, 1938, National Archives, Minden Post Office file.

74 Edward B. Rowan to Eugene Trentham, March 4, 1938, National Archives, O'Neill Post Office file.

75 Kenneth Evett to Edward B. Rowan, July 17, 1941, National Archives, Pawnee City Post Office file.

76 Ibid., February 20, 1942.

77 Ibid., Carl Eric Linden to Edward B. Rowan, March 5, 1942, and Kenneth Evett to Edward B. Rowan, March 7, 1942.

78 Edward Bruce in Bruce and Watson, *Art in Federal Buildings,* 289.

79 Edward B. Rowan to Louis Pelzer, February 24, 1939, National Archives, Minden Post Office file; Edward Bruce in Bruce and Watson, *Art in Federal Buildings,* 284; essay by Eugene Trentham in O'Connor, *Art for the Millions,* 133.

80 "Speaking of Pictures," *Life*, December 4, 1939, 12–13.

81 Ibid., 13; Marling, *Wall-to-Wall America,* 84.

82 Marling, *Wall-to-Wall America,* 222–23.

83 Park and Markowitz, *Democratic Vistas,* 16.

84 *Bulletin Number 18* (Section of Fine Arts, February 1939), 4.

85 Edward Bruce to G. Glenn Newell, September 25, 1940, National Archives, Crawford Post Office file.

86 Edward B. Rowan to Kenneth Evett, March 11, 1942, National Archives, Pawnee City Post Office file.

87 Ibid., Kenneth Evett to Edward B. Rowan, May 11, 1942, and Edward B. Rowan to Kenneth Evett, May 19, 1942.

88 Park and Markowitz, *Democratic Vistas,* 7–8. Marling estimates the number of murals at 1,116 with an additional 89 credited to the Treasury Relief Art Project. See Marling, *Wall-to-Wall America,* 211.

89 "Government Inspiration," 42.

A Folio of Nebraska Post Office Murals

1 *Pikes Peak Vision: The Broadmoor Art Academy, 1919–1945* (1989), 65. Catalog of exhibition at the Colorado Springs Fine Arts Center.

2 "Boston of the West," *Time*, April 27, 1936, 54. The building received acclaim for its architect, John Gaw Meem.

3 Oral interview with Kenneth Evett, October 10, 1964; Archie Musick, *Musick Medley*, 93.

4 Edward B. Rowan to Jenne Magafan, September 16, November 29, 1938, National Archives, RG 121, Entry 133, Box 61 (hereafter National Archives), Albion Post Office file.

5 Ibid., May 4, June 20, 1939.

6 Ibid., Jenne Magafan to Edward B. Rowan, July 2, 1939, G. M. Gaskill to Edward B. Rowan, July 12, 1939; "As the Public Pulse Beats," *Omaha World-Herald*, July 7, 1939, 12.

7 "Denver Mural Painters Gain Distinction," *Rocky Mountain News*, June 1, 1941, 15; Steve Frangos, "The Twined Muses: Ethel and Jenne Magafan," *Journal of the Hellenic Diaspora* 31, no. 2 (2005).

8 Edward B. Rowan to Ethel Magafan, July 23, 1937, National Archives, Auburn Post Office file.

9 Interview with Ethel Magafan, November 5, 1964, Archives of American Art, Smithsonian Institution.

10 Edward B. Rowan to Ethel Magafan, September 27, 1937, National Archives, Auburn Post Office file.

11 Ibid., Ethel Magafan to Edward B. Rowan, November 28, 1937, Edward B. Rowan to Ethel Magafan, December 8, 1937, March 7, 1938.

12 Ibid., Mrs. H. G. Harris to Treasury Department Procurement Division, July 14, 1938; Edward B. Rowan to Mrs. H. G. Harris, July 19, 1938.

13 Frangos, "The Twined Muses."

14 G. Glenn Newell to Edward B. Rowan, March 20, 1940, National Archives, Crawford Post Office file.

15 Ibid., Edward B. Rowan to G. Glenn Newell, August 22, 31, 1939, G. Glenn Newell to Edward B. Rowan, August 24, 1939.

16 Ibid., Edward B. Rowan to G. Glenn Newell, October 13, 1939.

17 Ibid., G. Glenn Newell to Edward B. Rowan, January 3, 1940, Edward B. Rowan to G. Glenn Newell, March 12, 1940.

18 Ibid., G. Glenn Newell to Edward B. Rowan, March 20, 1940.

19 Ibid., March 27, 1940.

20 *Northwestern Nebraska News* (Crawford), May 9, 16, 1940.

21 Ibid., May 16, 1940.

22 Edward Chavez to Edward B. Rowan, November 14, 1941, National Archives, Geneva Post Office file.

23 Ibid., March 2, 1941; Edward Chavez to Carol A. Ahlgren, March 20, 1991, Nebraska State Historical Society (hereafter NSHS), State Historic Preservation Office (FM06-126).

24 Edward B. Rowan to Edward Chavez, March 12, 1941, National Archives, Geneva Post Office file.

25 Ibid., June 13, 1941.

26 Ibid., Edward Chavez to Edward B. Rowan, September 26, 1941, George Koehler to Public Works Agency, October 7, 1941.

27 Edward Chavez to Carol A. Ahlgren, March 20, 1991, NSHS; Jacinto Quirate, *Mexican American Artists* (Austin: University of Texas Press, 1973), 58.

28 Oral history interview with Edward Chavez, November 5, 1964, Archives of American Art, Smithsonian Institution.

29 "Beautiful Mural Now Adorns Postoffice Lobby," *Hebron Journal*, November 23, 1939.

30 Eldora Lorenzini to Edward B. Rowan, November 7, 1938, Edward Rowan to Eldora Lorenzini, November 26, 1938, National Archives, Hebron Post Office file.

31 Ibid., Eldora Lorenzini to Edward B. Rowan, January 14, 1939.

32 Ibid., Edward B. Rowan to Eldora Lorenzini, January 20, 1939; "Beautiful Mural Now Adorns Postoffice Lobby."

33 Forbes Watson to Eldora Lorenzini, March 23, 1939, Edward B. Rowan to Eldora Lorenzini, March 27, 1939, Eldora Lorenzini to Edward B. Rowan, June 12, 1939, National Archives, Hebron Post Office file.

34 Ibid., Edward B. Rowan to Eldora Lorenzini, June 20, 1939, Eldora Lorenzini to Edward B. Rowan, June 29, 1939.

35 Ibid., Edward B. Rowan to Eldora Lorenzini, July 25, 1939.

36 Ibid., August 24, 1939.

37 Ibid., October 11, 1939.

38 Ibid., Eldora Lorenzini to Edward B. Rowan, January 17, 1940.

39 Elizabeth Anderson, "Depression Legacy: Nebraska's Post Office Art." *Nebraska History* 71, no. 1 (Spring 1990): 23–33.

40 William E. L. Bunn to Edward B. Rowan, n.d., Inslee A. Hopper to William E. L. Bunn, August 19, 1937, National Archives, Minden Post Office file.

41 Ibid., William E. L. Bunn to Edward B. Rowan, December 5, 1937; William E. L. Bunn to Merrill Mattes, April 27, 1938, William E. L. Bunn Papers, Archives of American Art, Smithsonian Institution.

42 Edward B. Rowan to William E. L. Bunn, December 9, 1937, National Archives, Minden Post Office file.

43 Ibid., January 20, June 8, August 3, 1938, William E. L. Bunn to Edward B. Rowan, May 27, 1938.

44 Ibid., William E. L. Bunn to Edward B. Rowan, October 8, 1938.

45 Ibid., December 27, 1938.

46 Ibid., Emil Nelson to Section of Fine Arts, January 10, 1939.

47 "A Mural Placed in Post Office," *Minden Courier*, January 12, 1939.

48 Edward B. Rowan to William E. L. Bunn, August 5, 1939, National Archives, Minden Post Office file.

49 "Smithsonian Procures Bunn Collection," *Ojai Valley* (California) *News*, May 5, 2010, B4.

50 Edward B. Rowan to Frank Mechau, April 18, 1938, Frank Mechau to Edward B. Rowan, April 24, May 1938, National Archives, Ogallala Post Office file.

51 Ibid., Frank Mechau to Edward B. Rowan, June 28, 1938.

52 Ibid., Edward B. Rowan to Frank Mechau, August 9, 1938, Frank Mechau to Edward B. Rowan, September 6, 1938.

53 Ibid., Frank Mechau to Edward B. Rowan, October 2, 1938.

54 From a letter Mechau addressed to Frank Lloyd Wright. as quoted in *Pikes Peak Vision: The Broadmoor Art Academy, 1919–1945*, 88–89; Kirkland School of Art, Summer 1933 catalog.

55 Mechau was awarded Guggenheim fellowships in 1934, 1935, and 1938.

56 "Government Inspiration;" "Gentle Hogarth."

57 Frank Mechau to Edward B. Rowan, August 16, 1938, National Archives, Ogallala Post Office file.

58 From an essay by Eugene Trentham (1936) in Francis V. O'Connor, ed., *Art for the Millions* (Boston: New York Graphic Society, 1975), 132; Edward B. Rowan to Eugene Trentham, February 12, 1938, Eugene Trentham to Edward B. Rowan, June 24, 1938, National Archives, O'Neill Post Office file.

59 Ibid., Edward B. Rowan to Eugene Trentham, May 25, 1938.

60 Ibid., July 1, 1938, Agnes E. Sullivan to Edward B. Rowan, June 13, 1938; "Mural Painting Installed in Lobby of Post Office," *Holt County Independent* (O'Neill), June 17, 1938.

61 From an essay by Eugene Trentham (1936) in O'Connor, *Art for the Millions*, 132–33.

62 Kenneth Evett to Edward B. Rowan, n.d., National Archives, Pawnee City Post Office file.

63 As quoted in Karal Ann Marling, *Wall-to-Wall America* (Minneapolis: University of Minnesota Press, 1982), 213.

64 Edward B. Rowan to Kenneth Evett, November 1, 1941, National Archives, Pawnee City Post Office file.

65 Ibid., Kenneth Evett to Edward B. Rowan, n.d.; "New Mural Placed in Postoffice Lobby," *Pawnee Chief* (Pawnee City), June 10, 1942.

66 Oral interview with Kenneth Evett, October 10, 1964.

67 Musick, *Musick Medley*, 93; Archie Musick to Edward B. Rowan, January 15, 1940, National Archives, Red Cloud Post Office file.

68 Archie Musick to Edward B. Rowan, February 3, 1940, National Archives, Red Cloud Post Office file.

69 Ibid.

70 Ibid., February 10, 1940.

71 Ibid., Archie Musick to Maria K. Ealand, February 26, 1940.

72 Ibid., Edward B. Rowan to Archie Musick, March 15, 1940, Archie Musick to Edward B. Rowan, March 16, 1940.

73 Ibid., Archie Musick to Edward B. Rowan, May 6, 1940, Edward B. Rowan to Archie Musick, May 10, 1940.

74 Ibid., Edward B. Rowan to Archie Musick, July 13, 1940.

75 Ibid., April 12, 1941.

76 Ibid., C. H. Miner to Federal Works Agency, May 23, 1941; *Commercial Advertiser* (Red Cloud), April 25, 1941.

77 As quoted in Virginia Mecklenburg, *The Public as Patron*, 96.

78 Edward B. Rowan to Philip von Saltza, November 10, 1939, National Archives, Schuyler Post Office file; Jay McHale, "Philip von Saltza and His Maritime Art," *Sextant* 13, no. 1 (Fall 2004):17.

79 "'Wild Horse' Mural For Schuyler P.O.," *Schuyler Sun*, December 7, 1939. The other mural study, now in the collections of the NSHS, was possibly one submitted by Gladys Lux of Lincoln.

80 Edward B. Rowan to Philip von Saltza, November 10, 1939, National Archives, Schuyler Post Office file.

81 Ibid., August 26, 1940.

82 Ibid., Mary B. Farrell to Office of the Supervising Architect, September 6, 1940.

83 Ibid.

84 Sharon L. Gustafson, guest curator, Sheldon Memorial Art Gallery, *Early Nebraska Women Artists, 1880–1950*. Catalog from exhibition held September 14–December 30, 2001; "First All-Nebraska Mural for Valentine Postoffice," *Omaha* (Sunday) *World-Herald*, February 26, 1939, C:8.

85 Edward B. Rowan to Kady B. Faulkner, July 15, 1938, National Archives, Valentine Post Office file.

86 Section of Painting and Sculpture, *Bulletin Number 14* (July 1937-January 1938), 4; "Miss Faulkner Commissioned To Do Murals for Valentine Postoffice," *Cherry County News* (Valentine), June 23, 1938; *Bulletin Number 17* (Section of Painting and Sculpture, September 1938), 13.

87 Edward B. Rowan to Kady B. Faulkner, June 22, 1938, National Archives, Valentine Post Office file; "Prepares for a Mural Painting" (Valentine) *Republican*, July 8, 1938.

88 Edward B. Rowan to Kady B. Faulkner, July 15, 1938, National Archives, Valentine Post Office file.

89 Ibid., August 30, 1938.

90 "Historical or Allegorical?" (Valentine) *Republican*, February 24, 1939.

91 Ibid.

92 "The Mural is Installed," *Cherry County News* (Valentine), April 13, 1939.

93 "Criticism of Mural Attracts Attention," (Valentine) *Republican*, March 10, 1939; "Postoffice Center of Interest, Both Inside and Outside," (Valentine) *Republican,* April 14, 1939.

94 "A Nebraska Mural," *Nebraska State Journal* (Lincoln), March 9, 1939, 8.

95 "Art Storm…Over Valentine," *Omaha* (Sunday) *World-Herald*," March 12, 1939, C:5; "Role of Modern Art in Field of Industrial Design Lauded," *Lincoln Star*, March 13, 1939, 10; Edward B. Rowan to Dr. Lester D. Longman, May 1, 1939, National Archives, Valentine Post Office file.

96 Kady B. Faulker to Edward B. Rowan, April 12, 1939, National Archives, Valentine Post Office file.

97 Marguerite Phelps to Treasury Department, April 18, 1939, National Archives, Red Cloud Post Office file.

98 Edward B. Rowan to Marguerite Phelps, May 1, 1939, National Archives, Valentine Post Office file.

99 Ibid., Edward B. Rowan to Kady B. Faulkner, May 1, 1939,

100 Sharon L. Kennedy, "Nebraska Women Artists 1880–1950," *Nebraska History* 88, no. 3 (Fall 2007):89; Phil Kovinick and Marian Yoshiki-Kovinick, *An Encyclopedia of Women Artists of the American West* (Austin: University of Texas Press, 1988), 89–90; "U.N. Teacher Explains Move," *Omaha World-Herald*, July 3, 1950, 2; "Modern Art Explained," *Omaha Bee-News*, April 25, 1937, A6:2–3.

Selected Bibliography

Anderson, Elizabeth. "Depression Legacy: Nebraska's Post Office Art." *Nebraska History* 71, no. 1 (Spring 1990): 23–33.

Annual Report of the Secretary of the Treasury on the State of the Finances for the Fiscal Year Ended June 30, 1915. Washington, D.C.: Government Printing Office, 1916.

Annual Report of the Secretary of the Treasury on the State of the Finances for the Fiscal Year Ended June 30, 1937. Washington, D.C.: Government Printing Office, 1938.

Annual Report of the Secretary of the Treasury on the State of the Finances for the Fiscal Year Ended June 30, 1938. Washington, D.C.: Government Printing Office, 1939.

Archives of American Art, Smithsonian Institution. RG 121, microfilm reel DC29 (Nebraska).

Baigell, Matthew. *The American Scene: American Painting of the 1930's.* New York and Washington: Praeger Publishers, Inc., 1974.

Bruce, Edward, and Forbes Watson. *Art in Federal Buildings, Volume I.* Washington, D.C.: Art in Federal Buildings Inc., 1936.

Bunn, William E. L. Papers, Archives of American Art, Smithsonian Institution.

Contreras, Belisario R. *Tradition and Innovation in New Deal Art.* London and Toronto: Associated University Presses, 1983.

Evergood, Philip. "Concerning Mural Painting." In Francis V. O'Connor, ed. *Art for the Millions.* Boston: New York Graphic Society, 1975.

Frangos, Steve. "The Twined Muses: Ethel and Jenne Magafan." *Journal of the Hellenic Diaspora* 31, no. 2 (2005).

Gustafson, Sharon L. Guest Curator, Sheldon Memorial Art Gallery. *Early Nebraska Women Artists, 1880–1950.* Catalog from exhibition held September 14–December 30, 2001.

History of Post Office Construction, 1900–1940. United States Postal Service, Office of Real Estate, July 1982.

Interview with Ethel Magafan, November 5, 1964, Archives of American Art, Smithsonian Institution.

Kennedy, Sharon L. "Nebraska Women Artists 1880–1950." *Nebraska History* 88, no. 3 (Fall 2007), 62–95.

Keppel, Frederick P., and R. L. Duffus. *The Arts in American Life.* New York and London: McGraw-Hill Book Company, 1933.

Kovinick, Phil, and Marian Yoshiki-Kovinick. *An Encyclopedia of Women Artists of the American West.* Austin: University of Texas Press, 1988.

Marling, Karal Ann. *Wall-to-Wall America.* Minneapolis: University of Minnesota Press, 1982.

McDonald, William F. *Federal Relief Administration and the Arts.* Columbus: Ohio State University Press, 1969.

McHale, Jay. "Philip von Saltza and His Maritime Art." *Sextant* 13, no. 1 (Fall 2004).

McKinzie, Richard D. *The New Deal for Artists.* Princeton, N.J.: Princeton University Press, 1973.

Mecklenburg, Virginia. *The Public as Patron.* College Park, MD: University of Maryland, 1979.

Musick, Archie. *Musick Medley.* Colorado Springs: Creative Press Adv., Inc., September 1971.

National Archives. RG 121, Entry 133, Box 61. Contains post office files for each of the twelve Nebraska post offices that received murals.

Nebraska State Historical Society. State Historic Preservation Office (FM06-126).

O'Connor, Francis V., ed. *Art for the Millions.* Boston: New York Graphic Society, 1975.

Oral interview with Edward Chavez, November 5, 1964. Archives of American Art, Smithsonian Institution.

Oral interview with Kenneth Evett, October 10, 1964. Archives of American Art, Smithsonian Institution. RG121, microfilm reel DC29 (Nebraska).

Park, Marlene, and Gerald E. Markowitz. *Democratic Vistas: Post Offices and Public Art in the New Deal.* Philadelphia: Temple University Press, 1984.

Pikes Peak Vision: The Broadmoor Art Academy, 1919–1945 (Colorado Springs Fine Arts Center, 1989).

Quirate, Jacinto. *Mexican American Artists.* Austin, Texas: University of Texas Press, 1973.

Witte, Ernest F. "The Nebraska FERA Art Exhibit." *Nebraska History* 16, no. 1 (January-March 1935), 57–60.

Photographic Credits

Photos are listed by the page on which they appear. Where applicable, file or record group numbers are shown in parentheses.

Frontier Historical Society, Glenwood Springs, Colorado/Schutte Collection: 68

National Archives: 25 (121-GA-17-FAULKNER-KADY-1); 37 (121-PS-2488); 39 (121-GA-MAGAFAN-J-1-1); 41 (121-PS-1800); 45 (121-PS-4117); 46 (121-GA-39-NEWELL-G-1-5); 47 (121-GA-39-NEWELL-G-1-3); 49 (121-GA-9-CHAV-2-4); 50 (121-GA-9-CHAV-2-3); 51 (121-PS-7885); 53 (121-GA-34-LORE-3); 54 (121-GA-34-LORE-5); 56 (121-GA-34-LORE-1); 57 (121-GA-34-LORE-2); 60 (121-PS-1633); 71 (121-PS-1691); 73 (121-PS-8412); 78 (121-GA-39MUSICK2-1); 79 (121-PS-4918); 82 (121-PS-5188, 121-PS-5189); 85 (121-GA-55VONSALTZA3-1); 89 (121-PS-22217); 91 (121-GA-17-FAULKNER-KADY-3)

Nebraska State Historical Society: Cover (H673-5 4859); viii (detail of H673-5 4898); 4 (743p-090); 7 (743p-001-02); 8 (743p-076); 9 (743p-076); 11 (RG4290-0103); 21 (H673-5 4884); 22 (RG2105-3-29); 24 (11055-1571); 36 (H673-5 4884); Plate 1, following p. 37 (H673-5 4888); 40 (RG2304-1-40); Plate 2, following p. 41 (H673-5 4859); 44 (RG3340-4-21); Plate 3, following p. 45 (H673-5 4882); 48 (RG3360-3-45); Plate 4, following p. 49 (H673-5 4908); 52 (RG2719-8-99); Plate 5, following p. 53 (H673-5 4913); 58 (RG2100-3-28); Plate 6, following p. 59 (H673-5 4918); 64 (RG2105-3-29); Plate 7, following p. 65 (H673-5 4903); 70 (RG3841-5-15); Plate 8, following p. 71 (H673-5 4863); 72 (RG2367-4-21); Plate 9, following p. 73 (H673-5 4898); 76 (RG1543-5-131); 77 (H673-5 4877, H673-5 4878); Plate 10, following p. 77 (H673-5 4876); 80 (H673.5-4871); 84 (RG3466-4-29); Plate 11, following p. 85 (H673-5 4869); 88 (RG3314-8-48); Plate 12, following p. 89 (H673-5 4893)

File numbers beginning with H673-5 indicate post office photos taken by Jeffrey Beebe for the NSHS in 1989.

Ethel Magafan estate: 42; 43

Paula Mechau estate: 34; 35; 65; 66

Smithsonian American Art Museum, Transfer from the General Services Administration: 74 (1982.86.3)

William Edward Lewis Bunn papers, Archives of American Art, Smithsonian Institution: 27; 59; 62; 63

Index